IMPLOSION

IMPLOSION

when the pendulum swings too far

ANN E. GILLIES, PH.D.

contents

foreword   vii

1   Black Is White & White Is Black   3

2   Every Colour of the Rainbow+   11

3   Kayla Lemieux   29

4   Pornography Saturation   37

5   Furries & Other Creatures   43

6   Pedophilia, the Crisis We're   53
      Not Discussing

7   Body Mutilation & the Medicalization   61
      of Children

8   The Buck Stops Here   67

9   Child Sexual Abuse   77

10 Dignity, Respect, & Identity   91

references   95
notes   103

foreword

AFTER A SPEAKING EVENT on the subject of gender and sexuality, a young man approached me to ask a few questions and share his story. I couldn't erase from my mind his concerns for our education system and the picture of what is happening. It lit a fire inside me.

For several years I have been attempting to raise awareness of the extremes of an ideology that knows no bounds. My words seemed to have been falling on deaf ears, until now. Parents, grandparents, and teachers are awakening slowly. The more they scratch the surface, the more appalled they become. There is currently a flood of parents removing their children from public education.

So what's happening? What has changed?

In *Implosion* you will find some of the answers. When the pendulum swings too far, there is bound to be a correction.

I believe we are on the verge of this correction. We haven't arrived yet, but perhaps this book will increase the momentum of change and, in doing so, help you throw a lifeline to our children.

1

Black Is White &
White Is Black

1

Black Is White &
White Is Black

How well I remember my mother saying to me, "Some people would argue black is white!" She was meaning, of course, that people would argue for their position, their ideas and opinions, even when the truth was staring them right in the face.

We have now entered an era where people not only fight for their position no matter the reality, but also everyone else must wholeheartedly agree with their delusions or suffer the consequence of being socially ostracised.

Last week I met a local teacher—a lovely forty-something black man, gracious, courteous, intelligent, and well able to separate truth from lies. Yet this man was in a quandary as to how to handle an ongoing situation at his elementary school.

He described the situation he was confronted with at the school where he works, just a half hour away from where I live. The situation concerned another teacher, a white male. These men are friends, but the white teacher recently decided to identify as a black man, putting a strain on the relationship and leaving the "true" black man exasperated.

> *You heard it right.*
> *White is the new black.*

I asked my new friend how he felt about this other teacher's assertion. He stood looking at me for a few moments, then shook his head, at a loss for words to describe his feelings—and, in our present politically correct climate, fearful to *express* his feelings due to possible repercussions.

I then remarked how I would feel if I were in his place—offended and challenged to explain the difference between black and white, not only chromosomally, but also racially and experientially. I heard an extended sigh of relief. Finally, he was talking to someone who got it, got him—someone who understood his confusion, his frustration, and his fear for the future of our children who are being exposed daily to such preposterous ideas.

This man's emotions are what most of us across North America are experiencing as we listen to the ridiculous notions being not only presented but also adamantly proclaimed as truths to be celebrated—ideas that have no basis in reality, yet support the insidious gender ideology.

Ideas such as

- A person can be born in the wrong body
- A boy can become a girl, and vice versa
- It's good to prescribe life-altering and harmful drugs to pre-pubescent children
- It's reasonable to lop off breasts and/or genitals
- It's educational to invite drag queens in full regalia denigrating women to read to a kindergarten class

These radical ideas are just the tip of the iceberg of ideas currently being marketed to our culture as good, wholesome, non-judgmental, inclusive, loving, kind, and, most important, necessary. Necessary for what? is the question.

So I ask you...why, after being systematically beaten over the head with all the media and political progressivism, are we shocked that someone would declare they are a different race? This white teacher is not the first to identify as black. These ideas have been hitting the news for nearly a decade.

In 2016, the leader of the National Association for the Advancement of Colored People, Rachel Dolezal, declared, "I identify as black," even though she was born white. Dolezal did not deny her biological parents are Caucasian. She admits to being of Czech, German, and Swedish descent. She doesn't deny that she has changed how she looks at herself over the years and admits to not having corrected various published reports over the years labelling her as transracial, biracial, and black.[1]

What adults do to or with their bodies is their personal decision, their choice, right? They're not hurting anyone else, right? That's how the argument goes, but let's get real. Sure, they can do whatever they like, but there are ramifications that have far-reaching consequences, not only for them, but also for everyone in society.

The University and College Union in the United Kingdom stated in 2019 that, regardless of skin tone, people should be able to say if they identify as black.[2] The union, which represents 120,000 academics, set out its stance after facing criticism over the labelling of transgender people, saying the union supports self-identification in a variety of areas.

Read this again. A **union of university and college educators** publishes a statement that is nothing more than an outright lie. Of course, gender-theory lies have been circulating for decades, but this statement clearly shows the depth of corruption in academia. What the universities adopt as truth *becomes* "truth" for entire generations.

This organization stated:

> Our rules commit us to ending all forms of discrimination, bigotry and stereotyping. UCU has a long history of enabling members to self-identify whether that is being black, disabled, LGBT+ or women.[3]

I don't *identify* as a woman; I am a woman by biological design! And what about the truly disabled? They don't *identify* as disabled; they have medical proof they are disabled. How disingenuous to minimize the truth in order to placate those who promote deceptive ideologies.

The union then added:

> UCU also **supports a social, rather than a medical, model of gender recognition** that will help challenge repressive gender stereotypes in the workplace and in society [emphasis mine].[4]

Hello! Universities supporting a social rather than a medical model? This has nothing to do with accurate, verifiable research, but rather an educational and political agenda as well as a social contagion.

Calling a white person black, a male a female, a mother a father, a child a cat, is deception, plain and simple. Academics, politicians, media personnel, are not only deceiving themselves, but they are also causing a mass confusion and psychosis in our society that blurs reality. We have a mentally confused culture, creating mentally ill people.

Worst of all, these assertions harm children. Our most vulnerable are being brainwashed into believing lies. The continued bombardment of false information is literally changing the brains of our children. New neurological pathways are being formed in order to accommodate this novel and very damaging information. In the process, children's minds, which instinctively know these claims are not truth, are reeling in an attempt to grasp what is right and what is wrong. These children, under constant verbal attack and emotional abuse in our schools, have little choice: they either succumb to the lies and "go with the flow," numbing their cognizance; shut down completely; or silently object and quietly keep their heads down. The only other option is speaking out, but as we've seen in Canada, there is a high cost to challenging the narrative.

In order to survive in the public school system and maintain any level of sanity, it is imperative that children just give in to these lies. They have to pretend to go with the flow and declare themselves by a false identity: for example, bisexual, biracial, alien, or, coming soon, transhuman.

This is the new road to be traveled with least resistance. And those who succumb to "transitioning" to something other than what or who they are entering a new level of mental illness never experienced before in history. And they must fervently support their delusions with aggressive, hate-filled rhetoric aimed at anyone who would challenge their perceptions or in any way disagree with them.

2

Every Colour of
the Rainbow+

2
Every Colour
of the Rainbow+

The word *gay* has been used now for decades in an attempt to replace the more descriptive word *homosexual*. The term *homosexual* is descriptive of a specific type of sexual behaviour: men having anal intercourse (previously called sodomy) with other men. While *homosexual* is the proper descriptive term, it is not the word picture the homosexual community wishes to paint.

Half a decade ago, to be gay meant to be happily excited. Gay meant to be merry, cheerful: "in a gay mood"; being "keenly alive and exuberant" or having high spirits.[5] Now there is an alternative meaning; in fact, we are usually hesitant now to use the word in its original form. Instead it refers to "characterized by sexual or romantic attraction to people of one's same sex"; e.g., gay men.[6]

The repositioning of the word *gay* was strategic. It succeeded in making homosexuality more acceptable to the general public. Gay is now used to depict a behaviour that initially causes pain and over time collapses the muscles of the rectum. The practice of men having sex with men precipitates many sexual diseases, cancers, and early death.

Health concerns for this small minority of the population are vast.[7] Relationships have been demonstrated between anal intercourse and anal cancer in gay men.[8] The Centers for Disease Control 2001–2006 indicated that young men who have sex with men were the only risk group with an increasing number of HIV/AIDS diagnoses; the increase was an alarming 93% among young black men.[9]

According to a 2009 Canadian study, the documented life span of the average homosexual male is about twenty years shorter than that of the general public. The study found that life expectancy at age 20 for gay and bisexual men ranged from 34 to 46 years and estimated that nearly half of gay and bisexual men would not reach their 65th birthday.[10] Physical and mental health among LGBT individuals is far more compromised than many are prone to acknowledge.[11] Minimizing these statistics puts this group of people at further risk. How can a sexual behaviour that causes such health risks be considered *gay*?

Have you ever wondered about the meaning of some of the colours of the LGBTQ+ flag and what our country and affirming nations of the world are celebrating? I'm about to explain, and let me tell you, we all have a lot to learn. Let's start with the easy part first.

According to Butler and Grace (2018), "the abbreviation LGBT stands for lesbian, gay [homosexual], bisexual, and transgender." These terms started to be used in the 1990s. The LGBT acronym was created as a way to describe people with different sexual orientations and has been "adopted into the mainstream as an umbrella term" for sexuality and gender.[12]

The six-colour rainbow flag (red, orange, yellow, green, blue, and purple) was "originally introduced by Gilbert Baker in 1978 and has commonly been used as a way of showing identity or support."[13] We now have flags with added colours to show support for the following identities.

- Six-colour rainbow – Lesbian, gay, bisexual, and transgender
- Blue/Purple/Hot Pink – Bisexual (person who is sexually attracted to both men and women)
- Blue/Yellow/Hot Pink – Pansexual (person who is not limited in sexual choice about biological sex, gender, or gender identity)
- Purple/White/Grey/Black – Asexual (person who does not have sexual feelings or attractions)
- Purple/White/Green – Genderqueer (person who identifies with neither, both, or a combination of male and female genders)
- Green/Brown/Blue – Sapiosexual (person who finds intelligence sexually attractive or arousing)[14]

Oh, baby, we've come a long way from Noah's ark. But we are far from done yet. The language around gender and sexuality is exploding. As my dad would say, it's...ed-ja-meca-tion time! Let's begin.

Chelette (2023) offers this information regarding "navigating gender identity": "Genderfandom.com lists over 700 possible gender identities, complete with flags and often pronouns. Sexualdiversity.org currently lists 94 gender identities. Male and Female are considered archaic social constructs that restrict human flourishing."[15] I have provided just a few of those identities. To see their corresponding flags in full color you can visit https://queerintheworld.com/different-lgbtq-flags-and-meaning/ or they are visible in the eBook edition.

———————

ANDROPHILIA: This flag depicts the love of men; a "sexual attraction to men or masculinity" by people of any sex or gender.[16]

ANDROGYNOUS: A person having "characteristics or nature of both male and female" or reversing traditional male and female roles.[17]

ASEXUAL: An asexual individual is someone who feels little or no sexual attraction.

AUTOSEXUAL: This is when one "experiences sexual attraction primarily or exclusively towards oneself." It can occur in different forms such as a person who has difficulty responding to another's sexual touch, but is comfortable with self-pleasing (masturbation).[18] Experiencing romantic feelings towards oneself is called *autoromantic*.

AROMANTIC: An aromantic has little or no romantic feeling toward others, or experiences little or no romantic desire or attraction.

BISEXUALITY: Characterized by a sexual or romantic attraction to both the same sex and the opposite sex.

BEAR: This newer term is used for homosexual men who exhibit "a specific set of physical traits," such as a large, sturdy build and facial and body hair.[19] The image of a bear in this context is of a man who exemplifies masculinity in a rugged sense of the word.

There are other terms attributed to men who have sex with men that derive from the animal concept. One of these is **cub**. The name *cub* in LGBT terms means a young man. The original meaning in nature is a **baby bear**.

BDSM PRIDE: The bondage and sadomasochism flag looks almost identical to the gynephilia flag but the meaning is entirely different. BDSM stands for bondage, domination, sadism ("deriving sexual gratification from inflicting [physical] pain or emotional abuse"; "extreme cruelty"),[20] and masochism (deriving sexual gratification from allowing oneself to be physically or emotionally abused).[21]

According to the Merriam-Webster dictionary, BDSM is a sexual activity involving practices that use physical restraints, "the granting and relinquishing of control" over the person, and "the infliction of pain."[22] Simply put, it's all about domination and control. BDSM is considered to be part of *kink* or *kinking*.[23] *Kink* refers to any unusual taste in sexual behaviour. Behaviour in this category used to be considered deviant and abnormal. Now it's celebrated.

DEMIROMANTIC: This describes a person who is "romantically

attracted only to people with whom they already have an emotional bond."[24]

GENDER BINARY: Heterosexual or "straight" individuals (now called cisgender) have their own flag! I wasn't aware of the need for one, but nevertheless, here it is. Gender binary refers to those that believe there are only two sexes, male and female.

GENDER FLUID: These are individuals who declare gender identity is not fixed, but instead it is fluid, meaning it fluctuates depending on mood and circumstance. Sometimes individuals call themselves queer or question, but gender fluid have decided that they are not relegated to a particular label.

GENDER NONBINARY: This is an umbrella term to describe any gender identity that does not fit into a biological male and female identity. These people describe themselves as not exclusively man or woman, having no gender, and fall on a gender spectrum somewhere between male and female, or identify as totally outside binary gender identities.[25]

Before I continue with the flags, I want to explain a little about Alfred Kinsey (1984–1956). Kinsey made many false allegations in his famous study (1949). He used his "random sample" of 4,120 men, included nearly 1,000 present and former inmates (25%), many of whom were homosexuals and/or pedophiles.[26] From this biased sample, Kinsey determined that "37% of the total male population [in the U.S.] has...some sort of overt homosexual experience" and

KINSEY SCALE

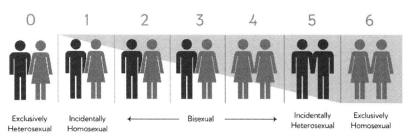

| 0 | 1 | 2 | 3 | 4 | 5 | 6 |

Exclusively Heterosexual | Incidentally Homosexual | ← Bisexual → | Incidentally Heterosexual | Exclusively Homosexual

Image found at steemit.com; copyright holder unknown.

13% of the population was predominantly homosexual.[27] However, studies in six different nations from 1987 to 2002 show that only 3.1% of men and 3.3% of women *have ever had* a homosexual experience in their entire lives—even if it was only one such experience.[28] For more information on Kinsey, the LGBTQ, and the indoctrination of our children, see *Closing the Floodgates: Setting the Record Straight on Gender and Sexuality.*[29]

GREY-ROMANTIC: Grey-romantics infrequently experience romantic attraction, although it is considered a weak attraction. Even if they are attracted, they may not desire a relationship or may only find attraction in specific circumstances.[30]

GYNEPHILIA: This is the opposite of androphilia (the love of men). Gynephilia represents someone who is attracted to femininity: a sexual attraction to women and female characteristics. Either men or women can be gynephilic.

HERMAPHRODITE: This is an older term used to describe a person in whom the sexual characteristics of both sexes are, to some extent, combined. These individuals are more often called *intersex*.

INTERSEX: The term used for a person who has underdeveloped male and/or female sex characteristics. This term encompasses several different diagnostic criteria for a biological anomaly. Characteristics of the disorder include genitalia, hormones, chromosomes, and reproductive organs. Being intersex is not a disease. It is extremely rare, and occurs in pre-birth development. Having an intersex condition is a medical diagnosis, **NOT an identity.**

LIPSTICK LESBIAN: This is a term used for a woman who is sexually attracted to other women who dress in a traditionally feminine manner. This is "a lesbian who has glamorously feminine characteristics," as opposed to the stereotypically masculine lesbian.[31] A lipstick lesbian, strictly speaking, is attracted to feminine women.

NEUTROIS: According to Gender Wiki, having a null or neutral gender, not male, female, or androgynous, but possibly genderqueer. Neutrois is associated with genderlessness, and shares many similarities with agender.[32]

PANSEXUAL: This person is characterized by "sexual or romantic attraction that is not limited to people of a particular [sex,] gender identity, or sexual orientation."[33]

POLYSEXUAL: A polysexual person is "someone who is sexually and/or romantically attracted to multiple genders." This is a separate designation from being bisexual or pansexual, even though "these sexualities involve being attracted to more than one [sex or] gender." Apparently being polysexual is not the same as being polyamorous.[34]

POLYAMOROUS: According to Flagwix, "the poly flag features three horizontal colored stripes of equal width, from top to bottom: blue, red, and black." In the center is "a gold Greek letter *pi*." It represents the first letter in *polyamory*.[35]

This flag represents relationships in which people date multiple partners or have romantic (and/or sexual) relationships with more than one individual at the same time. For polyamory to work, it must be based on the consent of all the people involved. Handling multiple romantic and sexual affairs at the same time sounds like a road to disaster!

SKOLIOSEXUAL: A skoliosexual is "sexually attracted to people who identify with a nonbinary gender" (they feel neither fully male nor fully female). According to the Gender and Sexuality Dictionary, "*skolio-* in *skoliosexual* comes from a Greek root meaning 'bent' or 'curved,' seen in the word *scoliosis*."[36] If you remember the root word, *bent* is also used when describing Kink alternatives.

STRAIGHT ALLY: Also referred to as "heterosexual ally." This is a heterosexual individual who supports equality for LGBT folk. They get involved in social movements and combat the concepts of homophobia, biphobia, and transphobia. "Despite this, some [of the] people who meet this definition do not identify themselves as straight allies." A straight ally *must believe that "LGBT people [constantly] face discrimination and thus are socially and economically disadvantaged."*[37]

STRAIGHT ALLY REDESIGN: This is the most current flag to represent allies. "Most LGBT organizations have [some] straight members involved [and] actively encourage straight participation. A gay–straight alliance [GSA] is a *student-run club*" required in all public education schools. The purpose is to "create a platform for activism" to promote homosexuality and the transgender identity.[38]

TRANSGENDER: Identifying as or having undergone medical treatment to attempt to become a member of the opposite sex. Individuals have used medical treatment, puberty blockers, hormones, and/or sex reassignment surgery in an attempt to align their biological sex with their gender dysphoria feelings.

The flags for transsexual and transgender appear to be one and the same.

TRANSSEXUAL: Transsexual is the word that transgender has replaced. "Transsexual people may or may not undergo surgery and hormone therapy to obtain a physical appearance typical of the gender they identify as."[39]

TWINK: The Twink flag doesn't have a set definition for each colour. It is assumed that the pink colour depicts more feminine or effeminate traits. The interlocking symbols in the center represent male-to-male sexual attraction.[40] Twinks are teen and adolescent men who have a slim physique and youthful appearance.[41]

THE PARAPHILIAS

BDSM

In the discussion about bondage and domination, I want to bring attention to the criteria for sexual masochism disorder and sexual sadism disorder found in the Diagnostic and Statistical Manual, fifth edition (DSM-V, also called the psychological bible).

The diagnostic criteria for sexual masochism disorder are intended for those who openly "admit having such paraphilic interests," acknowledging "intense sexual arousal from the act of being humiliated, beaten, bound, or otherwise made to suffer." If such individuals suffer "psychosocial difficulties because of their sexual attractions or preferences...they may be diagnosed" with this disorder. On the other hand, if they *do not feel distressed*, "they could be ascertained as having masochistic sexual interest, but *should not be diagnosed*" with the disorder.[42]

The diagnostic criteria for sexual sadism disorder applies both to those "who freely admit to having such paraphilic interests and to those who deny" such interests, despite "objective evidence to the contrary." Individuals reporting "intense sexual interest in the physical or psychological suffering of others" can be diagnosed with sexual sadism disorder. If "admitting individuals declare no distress, exemplified by anxiety, obsessions, guilt, or shame about these...

impulses," and "psychiatric or legal histories indicate they do not act on them, then they could be ascertained as having sadistic sexual interest," but not sexual sadism disorder.[43]

Transexual

Transsexualism was included for the first time in the Diagnostic and Statistical Manual, third edition (DSM-III) in 1980.[44] The eleventh revision of the International Classification of Diseases (ICD) was published in 2018 by the World Health Organization. This new revision of the ICD-11 has **abolished the codes** of *gender identity disorder* and *fetishistic transvestism*, among other sexual practices once considered as paraphilias.[45] These codes have been replaced in part by *gender incongruence*, which refers to conditions that classify under the term *gender dysphoria*.[46]

This is a major paradigm shift. Gender variant behavior and preferences alone are no longer a basis for assigning a gender identity disorder or gender dysphoric diagnosis. This shift has profoundly changed the way science and psychology view transgender people and transsexuals.[47] This shift in diagnosing has removed the stigma related to being referred to as people who "suffer from paraphilias."[48] I believe in doing so the DSM has unfortunately left such individuals adrift, like ships without a rudder, by neither providing an adequate diagnosis nor much needed psychological care. There are many comorbid mental illnesses observed in this group, including a large percentage of the gender dysphoric that fall within the autism spectrum.

Transvestic Disorder

One diagnosis still included in the DSM-V is transvestic disorder.[49] This disorder, observed primarily in men who cross-dress (e.g., drag queens), includes sexual fantasies and sexual urges, but must cause clinically significant distress. According to the DSM, transvestic disorder is often accompanied by *autogynephilia* (a man's tendency to be aroused sexually by the thought or image of himself as a woman).[50]

Autogynephilia

Autogynephilia was first identified by Toronto-based sexologist Dr. Ray Blanchard. To read more on this long-neglected aspect of transvestites, see Blanchard's autogynephilia theory.[51] Blanchard's extensive studies also include pedophilia and sexual orientation. Dr. Blanchard's works have been cited more than 14,000 times.[52] Nevertheless, autogynephilia is no longer addressed when treating the gender dysphoric. Blanchard has instead been thrown under the bus and reported by Southern Poverty Law as a far-right scientist and academic, associated with supposedly pseudoscientific theories![53]

Pedophilia

One last diagnosis that I want to quickly discuss while we are on the subject of paraphilias is that of pedophilia. It comes right after sexual sadomasochism in the DSM-V. While there are some who might take offense at my including this diagnosis here, I want to remind you that it is relevant to the conversation.

Pedophilic Disorder diagnosis can only be given if

- the individual has experienced six months of recurrent, intense, sexually arousing fantasies, sexual urges, or behaviours involving sexual activity with a pre-pubescent child or children
- has acted on these fantasies, or the urges and fantasies cause marked distress
- the individual is at least sixteen years of age and at least five years older than the child.[54]

If the individual is in late adolescence and "involved in an ongoing sexual relationship with a twelve- or thirteen-year-old," they are not considered eligible for the diagnosis.[55] The criteria for diagnosis are similar to transvestic disorder. The diagnosis applies to individuals who "freely disclose" and to individuals who "deny...sexual attraction to pre-pubescent children." Also if they report these attractions are "causing psychosocial difficulties, they may be diagnosed."[56]

"However, if they report an *absence of feelings of guilt, shame, or anxiety about these impulses* and are not functionally limited by their paraphilic [pedophilic] impulses," and their "recorded histories indicate that they have never acted on [such] impulses," these individuals have "a **pedophilic sexual orientation** but **not pedophilic disorder**"! [emphasis mine][57] Read this again. A pedophilic sexual orientation— what does that mean? After it's declared to be an orientation, it then becomes legal. Think of the phrase *born that way*.

If you thought the waters were getting muddied by all the colours under the rainbow and your mind was oversaturated, that was just the beginning. By now I expect you may feel like you're swimming in quicksand. I know that at times I feel this way. All the information is overwhelming. Imagine how our children must feel.

As this book was going to press, a friend sent me an article that revolted me and at the same time confirmed for me that **now is the time** for *Implosion* to be published. The article reported that a "gay bear mural" of a "a large hairy, naked man...with a teddy bear's head" appeared at a busy transit station in Sydney, Australia, prior to WorldPride 2023. Other instances of such "street art" were several murals featuring "a rainbow of phallic symbols" positioned at child height. The article reports that children were "pressured into being photographed" against a backdrop of such murals, and concluded, "Quietly and subtly, the kids are converted. If this isn't indoctrination, what is?"[58] Can there be any doubt that the gay agenda is targeting our children?

I believe we need to understand all that is being represented when we celebrate PRIDE. It seems to me there is a very fine line between *culturally "acceptable" deviance* and *unacceptable sexual behavior.*

Kayla Lemieux

3

Kayla Lemieux

The image of a biological man claiming to be a woman by the name of Kayla Lemieux has gone viral. Kayla's picture was taken during class hours while the teacher, teaching students how to use a circular saw, wore ludicrously oversized fake breasts.[59] Apparently he/she has been dressing this way for a considerable amount of time, which begs the question: "Why wasn't he/she stopped the moment he (oops, pronoun correction—*they*) walked through the front doors of Oakville Trafalgar High School?"

The answer to that question is found in the school's reply to the outrage of parents:

> [The school] recognizes the rights of students, staff, parents/guardians and community members to *equitable treatment* without discrimination based upon gender identity and *gender expression* [emphasis mine].
>
> We strive to promote a positive learning environment in

schools consistent with the **values of the HDSB [Halton District school board]** and to ensure a safe and inclusive learning and working environment for all students, staff and the community, regardless of race, age, ability, sex, gender identity, gender expression, sexual orientation, ethnicity, religion, cultural observance, socio-economic circumstances, or body type/size [emphasis mine].[60]

I reiterate: the **values of government paid employees, aka the school board***—not parental values or biological/medical absolutes. The word "absolutes" may raise hackles, but so be it. To deny the existence of absolutes is to deny the value of telling our children the truth.

*(While remuneration for service on a school board is not a universal practice, it occurs in some places in the U.S. and Canada, including Ontario.)

"Equitable" means to deal fairly and equally with all concerned. For sure this is a difficult balance to keep in our present day. After all, "Kayla" is a declared female, and as we know, the definition of "woman" has been subjugated to gender elite ideology. This means he/she must be protected at all costs, even to the diminishing and degradation of biological women.

I was repulsed when I saw "Kayla's" picture. It is offensive, demeaning, and as with all gender ideology, built on the theory of feeling and delusion. To think that he/she claims this as the image of a woman boggles the mind. It is absolutely degrading. "Kayla" (remember, "she" is a biological male) is an exhibitionist who craves the attention of young teen boys.

Such huge prosthetic breasts are primarily associated with "***computer-generated pornography***—in particular, what the Japanese call *bakunyuu* (爆乳) [Kay, 2022, emphasis mine]." I've included the link, but I don't suggest you look at it. *Bakunyuu* is nothing more than disgusting and denigrating porn. The word *bakunyuu* literally means "exploding milk/breasts, big boobs."[61] This pornography is the ultimate in extreme humiliation and belittling of women.

To suggest, as many gender ideologists do, that Kayla's image has nothing to do with porn or sexual grooming is absurd. It is pornographic, and you can bet Kayla is enjoying every minute of attention from the teen boys in the class. This case may seem extreme, but the whole public school system is intent on training children that there are no limits with sexuality and that pornographic images should not be challenged.

Now, there have been suggestions that Kayla is dressing like this as a way of highlighting the atrocities of the transgender delusion, but I have yet to see evidence of that. Also, if that were the case, one day on the premises would have been enough to highlight the issue; yet, to my knowledge, Kayla continues to come to class dressed in this way!

The new norm of "trans-women are women" states that "there is never any real difference between trans and biological women, except unimportant details arising from physiology" (Kay, 2022).

Don't get me wrong. As an adult, Lemieux is free to dress however he wants in his private life. But I heartily agree with Jonathan Kay when he states, "[The] sexualized clown outfit Lemieux is wearing is not something any actual (psychologically healthy) woman would wear to an ordinary workplace—let alone when working with children."[62]

Where I disagree with Kay is when he fails to acknowledge that such behaviour is preying upon children. He seems to be ignoring the effects of teen boys' hormones and/or fantasies and how easily boys are stimulated by what they see. I assert that Kayla's behaviour is an act of sexual grooming. This *teacher* is wearing "in your face" boobs that purposely promote a sexual response from young men. And this situation illustrates one of the reasons that schools should enforce dress codes.

Oakville Trafalgar High School's own website states that *"dress codes must prevent students from wearing clothing that exposes or makes visible genitals and nipples* [emphasis mine]." Imagine! The logic of why school board chair Shuttleworth declared the board's affirmation of Lemieux's outrageous paraphilia—i.e., "a pattern of recurring sexually arousing mental imagery or behavior that involves unusual and especially socially unacceptable sexual practices such as sadism or pedophilia"[63]—goes no further than the issue of gender rights.

The Halton District School Board has stood by the shop teacher, against parental concerns. Gender rights trumps every other right imaginable, and particularly rights of the child, parents, and women.

By defending Lemieux, the Oakville school board has put its stamp of approval on pornography, the devaluing of women, the sexualization of children, and general moral depravity.

Ontario Education Minister Steven Lecce stated, "In this province, in our schools, we celebrate our differences and we also believe that there must be the highest standards of professionalism in front of our kids."[64] So herein lies the dichotomy: how can we have "highest standards of professionalism" where we embrace the sexualization of children via so-called inclusivity?

> *What has a sexually free culture accomplished in our schools?*

According to research, the average sexual offender (let's call them predators) is involved with over seventy children in his or her "career" of offending.[65]

In Canada:

> "As a result of recent amendments to the Ontario College of Teachers Act, the College has revoked the certificates of individuals...found to be guilty of an act of professional misconduct consisting of, or including, sexual abuse of a student or a prohibited act involving child pornography."[66]

From 2008 through 2022 there were a **total of 600 teachers** whose teaching certificates were revoked. These individuals were charged with sexual offences against minors, and most were sentenced to jail time [emphasis mine].[67] The following graph shows the trajectory. While not a perfect upward incline, offences are definitely on the rise. These, of course, are the offences we know of. How many more are "swept under the rug"?

67 of these revocations happened in 2022

> *How many children need to be sexually abused by teachers before we consider this a crisis?*

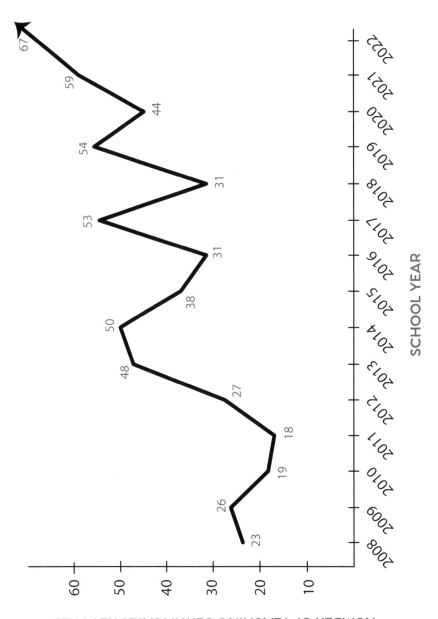

4

Pornography Saturation

4

Pornography Saturation

An article on the City, University of London website is titled "Four in five UK 16- and 17-year-olds have seen online pornography."[68] This 2021 study out of the United Kingdom found that "78% of respondents had seen online pornography on various platforms, and that their exposure was relatively recent."

The author, Chris Lines (2021), writes, "With the UK government looking...to protect children from online pornography, [this] new survey illustrates the size of the government's task....The results showed that more (63%) had seen pornography on social media platforms than on pornographic websites (47%)."

The study showed that these teens "spend an average of more than two hours a month on dedicated pornography sites.... Furthermore, the study found that 46% of 16- and 17-year-olds had used a virtual private network (VPN) or Tor browser."

Lines cites Neil Thurman, lead author on the study: "Until now, there was scant evidence on which media platforms and technologies children use to access pornography, and to what extent; this new survey fills that gap."[69]

Robert Weiss, a sex addiction therapist, gave a glimpse into online porn's devastating impact:

> Once the online world came about, it was a game-changer... I went from being a private clinician with one assistant, to running a clinic with eight therapists and 150 clients a week. I'm now seeing twenty-five-year-old men who've been looking at hard-core porn since they were fifteen, and never had a date.[70]

Pornography can derail a child's sexual development almost as quickly as childhood sexual abuse. "The brain can be molded positively by structure and guidance. It can also be molded negatively by poor input. What is certain is that the brain will be molded by one or the other" (McIlhaney and Bush, 2008).[71]

Current neurobiological research confirms that early sexual experience influences the developing brain of children and adolescents.[72] Each person changes the structure of their brain with the choices he/she makes. To quote Dr. Caroline Leaf, "Thoughts are measurable and occupy mental real estate."[73]

Your thoughts are active; as thoughts group, they begin to change neuropathways. As persistent thoughts grow and become more permanent, pathways extend, and the connections between brain structure, thoughts, and subsequent behavior strengthen.[74]

This means that the decades-old adage "garbage in/garbage out" is as relevant today as it was when coined. The only difference is there is a whole lot more garbage that our children are being exposed to on a daily basis. Not only are their brains being changed; they're being overheated!

My friend Jon Uhler has reviewed hundreds of criminal histories and interviewed thousands of men who have sexually offended. He confidently asserts that there is a 100% correlation between pornography and men who offend sexually. In other words, 100% of men who perpetrate sex offences will have been progressively accessing pornography for years **prior** to committing their sex offence. Additionally, 100% of all those men who have sexually offended a child will be charged with the possession of child pornography. Nearly all of the men with child victims will be charged with the distribution/dissemination of child pornography as well.[75]

The saturation of pornography changes the brain neurologically. What one fixates on can easily become an addiction. While viewing pornography in early years may seem innocuous, for many young men it becomes a serious addiction that escalates in an ever-increasing need for viewing new and more deviant experiences. It is a cumulative addiction that diminishes women and children into objects to be used for personal pleasure. One of the outlying consequences is then the need for personal gratification in the manner exemplified in the porn the individual has been looking at, leading to a violation of the unsuspecting person.

The progression and kind of pornography accessed by men who had progressed into pedophilia and child offending is deviant to the extreme. However, most academics who are producing "peer-reviewed" findings downplay the role of pornography in offending.[76,77,78] A growing number of academics applaud the use of pornography despite growing evidence of addiction and the reality of its effect on our culture.

5

Furries & Other Creatures

5

Furries & Other Creatures

Have you heard of the newest and greatest trend? If not, you're about to. *Furries* crawling in the halls of our government-sponsored schools came to my attention last summer. Within two weeks, five different sets of parents talked to me about their concerns and the rumors of kitty litter boxes being installed in school washrooms.

My first response was *Could the education system really have stooped this low*? A minute later: *Well, of course they could have.* As if identifying as newly invented "genders" was not bizarre enough, indoctrinated and confused children are now coming to class wearing tails, animal ears, collars, and even leashes.[79] Children are now crawling around our public schools dressed as cats (or dogs), meowing or growling and even in some cases biting other children.[80]

Apparently, teachers are expected to meow back when spoken to in this new foreign language. If teachers do not respond favourably, it is akin to rejecting a transgender child's preferred pronouns, which we all now recognize as the greatest slight ever imagined.

If men can identify as women and gain access to private areas intended for the opposite sex, there is no logical reason why students who identify as cats should not be provided litter boxes. To state the reality *"You are not a cat,"* to call the parents and send the child home, or to suggest that they seek psychological care would be considered an act of intolerance and judgment.

You cannot make up this level of craziness. Even legacy media are reporting on it.[81] It seems that the movement is growing. What began as adults—predominantly young white men—dressing as animals in Pride parades, and playing "dog and master"—a practice called PUPS (part of the KINK category)—has now expanded its demographics to children.

These adult males—nearly half are college students—have "an interest in computers and science, and a passion for video games, science fiction, fantasy, and anime."[82]

According to Merriam-Webster, *anime* is "a style of animation originating in Japan that is characterized by stark colorful graphics depicting vibrant characters in action-filled plots often with fantastic or futuristic themes."[83]

Believe it or not, there has been a decade of research on this subject. A team of researchers from the University of Waterloo tried to put a positive spin on it. The study indicates the LGBTQ demographics: "Furries are ***seven times*** more likely than the general population to ***identify as transgender*** and about ***five times*** more likely to ***identify as non-heterosexual*** [emphasis mine]."

The furry culture is "a community **defined...by its inclusivity**" that "**embraces [the idea] of being...non-judgmental to all** [emphasis mine]." This means that we must throw out any kind of discernment and once again accept delusions as reality.

Dr. Courtney Plante, social psychologist and co-founder of the International Anthropomorphic Research Project, suggests that the furry personalities created "typically consist of one or more animal species, a name, and personality traits or other characteristics....Furries are free to create representations of themselves unbounded by reality. As such, they can reconceptualize themselves [regarding] age, gender, personality, or physical characteristics."[84]

According to Plante,

> Research has shown that most furries create fursonas [animal personas] representing similar, but idealized versions of themselves. Many furries report that, over time, their own self-concept tends to become more like that of their animal persona. This may be due to the fact that, over time, others begin to interact with them as that idealized self, validating it and helping them to internalize it as part of themselves.[85]

This makes perfect sense from a psychological point of view. This is akin to creating the delusion that you are something (or someone) other than who you are in reality. The longer and more involved you are in the deluded state of mind, the more this state will become internalized. The more the state of mind is internalized, the more extreme the reactions and the need to defend the delusions.

This is **not** something to be celebrated. Delusions are dangerous. This is something that needs to be nipped in the bud. It is abusive to our children to collude with their delusions rather than speak truth. Unfortunately, our culture seems bent on promoting rather than preventing mental illness.

At the beginning of the 2021 school year, Camp Ernst Middle School in Kentucky sent the following notice to parents:

> We want to make you aware of some observations we have made this year regarding some behaviors and trends we are noticing that are different from prior years. We have noticed an uptick in TikTok trends such as challenges that encourage kids to destroy the soap dispenser in the bathroom and kids making animal noises toward each other, specifically barking.[86]

What the school found was that "social media outlets are...where these trends originate and circulate." Then the school set some boundaries around social behavior:

> We cannot allow kids to bark at each other or any other like behavior. We appreciate you helping us by discouraging such behaviors....In addition, we could also use your help regarding the clothing items these social media trends have inspired...that are not school-

appropriate such as collars...[and] leather straps with spikes which can be a safety concern.[87]

Kudos to this school for setting guidelines and calling parents to accountability. Perhaps it's time to implement school uniforms once again?

It seems that acceptance of the now-widespread belief that transgender people are "born in the wrong body" leaves the door wide open to accepting, applauding, and celebrating children defecating in litter boxes.

Straying from the dominant cultural narrative of "you are anything you think you are" can come at a cost to career, so educators and government officials have little choice but to encourage this behaviour.

PUPS

While "born in the wrong body" rhetoric is happening in our public schools, let me prepare you for what I believe are next steps. Children are now identifying as animals and crawling through the hallways of our schools. Although associated with the Furries phenomenon, it is far from harmless. Furries give way to other forms of deviancy.

Just a couple of years ago (I know I'm late to these deviant games) I came across something with a new twist. Pup play (or Puppy Play) is when one person takes on the role of a pup or handler.

Listen as Pup Gryphn explains. "I get down on all fours, I bark, I act like a dog. You adopt that mindset. 'Ooh, squirrel!' And suddenly you're chasing a squirrel for no reason at all. It's a lot of fun. It's good stress relief."[88]

Gryphn, 28, is one of a growing number of people taking part in puppy play. It's a deviance that grew out of the leather and BDSM communities and is often lumped in with other fetishes.

Gryphn's interest in "headspace" dates back to the early 2000s, when he was first introduced to the "furry" community, *a subset of the fetish and kink community* where people dress in costumes that have animal characteristics. "'Someone gave me the unique opportunity to wear the fur suit of a blue fox,' Gryphn says. 'That's when I learned what headspace is, adapting that character and moving forward with it.'"[89]

If you're new to BDSM (bondage, discipline, domination, submission, and sadomasochism), you might not yet have heard the term *headspace,* or one of its variations such as *sub-space, puppy-space, drop* and other such terms. What does this mean?

Headspace is generally considered to be an altered state of consciousness within BDSM. It means to "lose yourself" in a scene. This is a state of mind where the body's endorphins, enkephalins (compounds that occur naturally in the brain), and adrenaline take over the mind and *produce a morphine-like effect* [emphasis mine].[90]

These altered mind states help to convince the person to participate in sexual activities that they may not have ever been exposed to or considered. Essentially, the purpose of a scene is to lose oneself.[91]

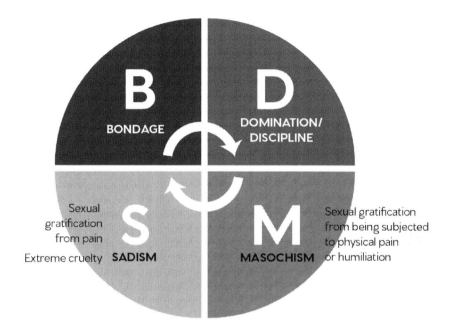

Permitting themselves to dissociate (which is what this state of mind is) allows these individuals to participate in risky, painful, and morally disturbing sexual practices such as urethral sounding, the use of inflating dildos, and anal stretching.

SUB-SPACE/PUPPY-SPACE

Caution: more disturbing material follows.

The submissive pup is usually aware of how they descended into a sub-space and they will remember that a major event has happened, but just as children dissociate under the effect of chronic sexual abuse, these men forget intimate details, or struggle to recall the majority of what happened during that state.[92] The dissociative state allows the brain to block painful memories, so that the individual forgets about the danger and risk, allowing them to immerse themselves within the scene in a trance.

The trance creates a state of strong relaxation, like a meditative or hypnotic trance, but it has the potential to grow deeper quickly. In this state, mental processes will be delayed or slowed. Therefore, the use of safety precautions like a pre-arranged "stop" signal might become difficult or even impossible to use in the deep trance. It is up to the dominant male to work out when a submissive person is in such a state and respond and react accordingly.[93]

It is frightening to think of the consequences when the dominator is unable or ill-equipped to bring the "pup" out of the trance and back into reality. This kind of sexual behavior is indeed torture. Adolescent boys are sometimes lured into PUP clubs by older men. If you've ever seen a PRIDE parade, you've probably seen adolescents and men in leather muzzles and skintight black rubber suits. These are examples of the PUP category.

If you believe that children identifying as furries is just a harmless phase, think again. This is simply one more identity meant to sexualize your child and groom them to accept all levels of sexual abnormalities.

6

Pedophilia,
the Crisis We're Not Discussing

6

Pedophilia, the Crisis We're Not Discussing

There are no typical pedophiles. They look no different from other people. These individuals do not carry signs declaring their deviance. They can be found in all professions, at all levels of society, and often hold respected and powerful positions in the community, coming from a variety of racial and religious backgrounds.

Pedophiles may act alone or organize themselves into groups which may operate within a local community, nationally, or internationally. In such groups, children and child pornography are passed among members. Such associations have gained momentum in recent years with the easy access of the internet and the relative safety from exposure it brings.

Pedophiles are often very good at making friends with children quickly and can appear warm and approachable. They often come across as "nice men." Women pedophiles are few and far between, although there seems to be an upsurge as women succumb to the lures of pornography, and women are often used by pedophiles to lure innocent victims into the web of the pedophile.

Perhaps the media coverage of Jeffrey Epstein and, later, the lack of coverage of Ghislaine Noelle Marion Maxwell's trial has served as a wake-up call to society. I certainly hope so.

According to Wikipedia, "Jeffrey Edward Epstein...was born and raised in Brooklyn, New York City, [and] began his professional life by teaching at the Dalton School in Manhattan," although he didn't have a teaching degree.

He deceptively "talked his way into a job at the Dalton School in 1974" and taught math and physics "to the children of wealthy New York families. It later emerged that he [had] lied on his job application to gain access to the girls at the exclusive academic institution" (Hodge, 2020).[94]

After being fired from teaching, Epstein "entered the banking and finance sector," becoming extremely successful. He "developed an elite social circle" and gained access to many women and children. Epstein and some of his associates then sexually abused them.[95]

> Epstein pleaded guilty [of sexual abuse] and was **convicted in 2008** by a Florida state court of procuring a child for prostitution and of soliciting a prostitute. He served almost 13 months in custody....He was convicted of only these two crimes as part of a controversial plea deal; federal officials had identified 36 girls, some as young as

14 years old, whom Epstein had allegedly sexually abused. Epstein was **arrested again on July 6, 2019**, on federal charges for **the sex trafficking of minors** in Florida and New York. He died in his jail cell on August 10, 2019 [emphasis mine].[96]

Although his death was ruled a suicide, the decision has been disputed by Epstein's lawyers. There has been much skepticism about the true cause of his death and many believe he was murdered by someone wanting to silence him. Epstein's long-time associate, the British socialite Ghislaine Maxwell, was convicted of **sex trafficking and conspiracy** in 2021. Maxwell helped Epstein lure girls, as young as 14, for child sexual abuse and prostitution.[97]

It seems incredible to me that high-profile men, including princes, politicians, and dignitaries, maintained long-term friendships with Epstein knowing he had previously been a convicted pedophile. Many of these men chose to accompany him to "Epstein Island." It takes a real stretch of the imagination to suppose they were simply innocent bystanders.

While sexual abuse of children remains a repulsive act in the minds of most people, pedophilia under the guise of **_"intergenerational intimacy"_** or **_"minor attracted persons" (MAPs)_** is gaining traction in our society due to a strong push from academia. The radicalization of terms and language is meant to soften the impact of the truth around the behaviour of pedophilia.

Here's the truth:

> MAP = *a pedophile*
> Sex with a minor = *rape—call it what it is*
> Underage woman/man = *a child*
> Non-consensual sex = *RAPE*

Academics now claim that most pedophiles first discover their attraction during puberty. These academics and "MAPs" believe that this attraction becomes *a central part of their identity*.[98] Sound familiar? Of course it does. Think LBG and the transgender ideology.

Remember the "born that way" mantra of the LGBT community? Then consider the not so new idea of pedophilic orientation! Yes, the psychological association (APA) that writes the "psychological bible" (DSM) attempted to have pedophilia declared an orientation in 2014. There were still enough conscientious professionals that stood in the way. I believe this is no longer the case, and the next edition of the DSM will likely declare that pedophiles also have an orientation. If this happens, pedophilia will no longer be criminalized.

Some researchers now suggest that "MAPs" with a same-sex attraction (homosexual desires for young boys) additionally experience a "second coming out" of sorts. This means these men who *identify as gay* then *realize they are gay and have an attraction to minors*.[99] MAPs often join online communities of like-minded individuals instead of "coming out" to people they know.[100]

One of the mottos of the LGBTQ movement is *too much is never enough*.

Years ago, sex researcher Alfred Kinsey suggested that "adult sexual contact" is ***good for the child***! We can only conclude that Kinsey considered child molestation, sexual abuse, or rape to be scientifically legitimate. For decades his conclusions went unchallenged. And these days an increasing number of academics *support* Kinsey's research and the idea that children need the help of older, more experienced persons to discover masturbatory techniques that are sexually effective.[101]

Schools that even a decade ago were considered a safe place for our children are no longer even on the safety radar. Teenage boys are allowed free access to girls' washrooms; bisexual (actually unisex) cabins are required for grade seven class trips, paving the way for twelve-year-olds to view other-sex nudity and more easily engage in sexual activity. Teachers such as the Ontario shop teacher are allowed to promote all types of sexuality in the classroom, without restriction.

Public schools now welcome members of the LGBTQ community to come into classrooms to teach children about inclusion and equality, without any thought of restriction or restraint. Child grooming proliferates in our schools. The curriculum is filled with pornographic art; drag queens read to kindergarten classes; children are encouraged to practice masturbation and given homework assignments that should make our blood boil. The result is that children, encouraged by peers and the classroom material that tells them that all sex is good, now assault other children on the playground and in the washrooms of our schools.

It's time to rise up, challenge lies about sexuality, and protect our children. Parents need to **take a stand** and **say no** to the craziness of absolute inclusivity. It amounts to nothing more than coaching children to receive sexual advances from anyone, making them easy targets for pedophiles.

Children don't need to be taught to consent. What they need to be taught is the art of **refusal.**

7

Body Mutilation & the Medicalization of Children

7

Body Mutilation & the
Medicalization of Children

Rolf Buchholz set a Guinness World Record for most body modifications—516. At sixty-two years of age, he says he isn't finished altering his body. Check out the website in the footnote below for pictures and the full article.[102] Call me judgmental if you wish, but this is plainly body mutilation. As an adult you are free to do what you like with your body, but don't expect others to find it appealing.

A few short years ago we would have been absolutely horrified with the thought of such mutilation, yet now young girls having their breasts removed seems almost commonplace. We would have appropriately felt saddened by such an event and quickly acknowledged that this child's life would be changed forever. Now we call it self-actualization, finding the true self. Breast removal might be justified as a treatment for aggressive cancer, but it should never be elective surgery for children.

Although breast cancer in teen girls is extremely rare and surgery almost non-existent, what is true is that young women with breast cancer who have mastectomies experience a persistent decline in their sexual and psychosocial well-being following the procedure.[103] They report a lower quality of life.

If these young women who had their breasts removed for legitimate medical reasons experience a lower quality of life, why would we assume that teens who are removing their breasts in order to fulfill a new social order would not have similar emotional experiences? The stark reality is that these are teens who already experience compromised and underdeveloped reasoning skills—a probable outcome of taking puberty blockers prior to puberty development. According to a group called Susceptible Minority, four teenagers in a detransition support group asked **how long it would take for their breasts to grow back!** Obviously, these teens skipped biology class.[104]

Most people fear the idea of losing a leg or an arm, or any other violation of the body's external form. Studies show we have a preserving behavior that is reduced in some individuals who desire the amputation of a healthy limb. Instead of actively avoiding body damage, some individuals share an urgency to permanently damage an apparently intact body.[105] This condition is called body integrity identity disorder (BIID).[106] It's a designated mental health diagnosis.

The first description of this disorder traces back to a series of letters published in 1972 in the magazine *Penthouse*. These letters were from erotically obsessed persons who wanted to become amputees themselves.[107]

BIID is rare (as was gender identity disorder until 2010). It's a condition where there is a mismatch between the mental body image and the physical body. This condition is characterized by an intense desire for amputation or paralysis of a limb, usually a leg, or to become blind or deaf. The person sometimes experiences sexual arousal connected with the desire for loss of a limb, movement, or sense.[108,109] Some BIID individuals act out their desires by pretending they are amputees and using prostheses or other tools to fulfill their desire to be an amputee, often using a wheelchair. This is a mental illness.

To the extent that generalizations can be made, people with BIID appear to start to wish for amputation when they are young, between eight and twelve years of age, and often knew a person with an amputated limb when they were children.[110] People with BIID seem to be predominantly male. There seems to be a correlation with BIID and a person having a paraphilia as well as a correlation with personality disorders.[111]

Michael First,[112] an American psychiatrist, published the first systematic attempt to describe individuals who desire amputation of a healthy limb. The process of amputation is the main focus of desire for these people. And why in the world would an individual choose to do such a thing?

According to research, there are several reasons.[113] I've listed some here along with the percent of individuals who disclosed their reasoning.

31% » *Because of attention it draws*

6% » *In order to be disabled and have others help me*

77% » *In order to feel whole, complete, set right again*

67% » *In order to feel sexually excited*

83% » *In order to feel satisfied inside*

Now we are being told we must celebrate the removal of healthy tissue in order to help the child validate their erroneous idea that they are born in the wrong body and therefore need to remove any part that doesn't fit their delusional experience. If we are doing this to children, why does the medical society deny the removal of healthy limbs for the BIID group?

Let's address the reality of children desiring to remove healthy body parts in order to attempt to "transition" to an opposite sex. They can never become the opposite sex biologically. Gender, remember, is simply a social construct—how we feel about our femininity or masculinity.

I believe that some of the same disturbed reasoning of those with BIID applies to gender dysphoric children.

8

The Buck Stops Here

8
The Buck Stops Here

Cultic brainwashing promoted by elites drives an irrational ideology in order to separate sex from stereotypical sex roles. According to Bilek (2022), we no longer talk of gender dysphoria, but rather about "expression," feelings, and "a journey" into the authentic self, who you really are—but let's not discuss biological sex.

This ideological cult is the new "religion devised to transform humanity" with "immense amounts of propaganda" (Bilek, 2022). It is heavily funded by billionaires. The Pritzker family are among the most prominent. They desire to "engineer the normalization of synthetic [sexual] identities through funding of our medical, legal, cultural, military, educational, and other institutions."[114]

Bilek notes that Yale University has received an influx of funding from the Pritzkers, with which they have created "a growing program in manufacturing synthetic sex."

According to Bilek (2022), "The University of Michigan has a neuro-psychology department bearing the Pritzker name," as well as a "gender clinic." Bilek says a "gender and sex development program" was opened at Lurie Children's Hospital in Chicago in 2013, "with a $500,000-$1 million gift pledge from Jennifer Pritzker."

In addition, in 2019 "the Pritzker Department of Psychiatry and Behavioral Health at Lurie [Children's Hospital] was launched with a $15 million gift from the Pritzker Foundation," and the department received "another $6.45 million in 2022." [115]

The average citizen has little to no awareness of the progressive infiltration into academia, medicine, and education that I have previously discussed, or the money being dumped into the degenerate implementation of the corruption of our children, but the agenda is beginning to surface. According to Woulahan (2022), "a gender clinic in Nashville, Tennessee, is now facing backlash after videos were posted to social media showing their top administrators describing gender surgeries as 'money makers.'" [116]

Recently, political commentator Matt Walsh published his hit documentary *What Is a Woman*, [117] exposing the extremes of the ideological revolution. I highly recommend you take the time to watch this. It is a pretty sorry state of affairs when people can't even tell you what a woman really is. In fact, if asked, some are even speechless.

If you are reading this book, it is unlikely that you are a member of the "woke" crowd. Therefore, you will not have succumbed to the idiocrasy of trying to figure out what a woman is; you would instinctively trust the explanations detailed in biology.

But I digress. The focus of gender ideology is money...money...

money. According to Woulahan (2022), "Vanderbilt University's Health Center opened its Clinic for Transgender Health in 2018." Also in 2018, "Dr. Shane Taylor gave a lecture [where] she described the explicit financial [opportunities] behind opening the gender clinic." She explained that "elective double mastectomies can '**bring in $40,000 dollars a patient**' [emphasis mine]." The surgery was declared a money-making project for the hospital.[118]

Take a moment and let's wrap our heads around that. The hospital makes $40,000 for each elective (meaning non-essential) breast removal per woman (or teen). Taylor stated that certain types of sex-change surgeries are "huge money-makers," especially because such surgeries require a lot of follow-up appointments.[119]

Another medical intervention favored by gender ideology is the use of puberty blockers to treat gender dysphoria. Two different drugs are used as puberty blockers. *Histrelin acetate* is administered as an implant that lasts for about a year. *Leuprolide acetate* is administered as an injection every one to four months.[120]

Leuprolide acetate, under the name Lupron Depot, is the puberty blocker most commonly used in British Columbia. Also used to treat cancer, the drug is quite expensive: about $400 a month in Canada.[121]

A form of the drug, Lupron Depot-Ped, is used for treating "central precocious puberty." It stops the body from "creating certain hormones, such as estrogen or testosterone," which in turn "[stops] certain cells from growing."[122] And this, of course, is why the drug is used as an elective puberty blocker.

The cost of puberty blocker injections is about $1,200 USD per month (close to $15,000 per year). For a puberty blocker implant, the cost is $4,500 to $18,000 USD.[5] At $15,000 per year, a ten-year-old put on puberty blockers for four years could cost health care (your tax dollars) $60,000 USD (approximately $81,666.00 CD). Sixty thousand dollars destroys a child's future.

The number of gender clinics treating children in the United States has grown quickly. The reputable Society for Evidence Based Gender Medicine estimates "as many as 300" have opened over "the past few decades."[123] The number of clinics has exploded in recent years while strong evidence of the efficacy and possible long-term consequences of that treatment remains scant.[124]

Euphemisms including "gender affirming care" and fun catchphrases like "Yeet the Teets" hide the permanent reality of young women getting double mastectomies. Once breasts have been removed, the ability to nurture a child has been lessened, with no ability to reverse the surgery.

According to Healthline, "The average range for cost of FTM [female to male]...top surgery is currently between $3,000 and $10,000 dollars. The average cost range for MTF [male to female]... top surgery varies greatly depending on factors such as body size, body shape, and desired breast size," but costs range between $5,000 and $10,000, and "there's typically a hospital or facility fee and an anesthesiologist fee added to the total bill."[125]

The profits that gender clinics rake in through offering vaginoplasties (a procedure to construct a vagina) are generous.

This procedure costs $20,000. This cost is only for one surgery. If the person wants a labiaplasty, costs increase as much as $5,000. According to Healthline, "Many who get vaginoplasties also undergo breast augmentation [$3,300–$9,800] and facial feminization surgeries [$10,000]." Added to this is the cost of electrolysis, usually in the thousands.[126]

The cost to attempt to become a woman is a ballpark figure of $44,800.00. This is if the surgeries are successful and recovery uncomplicated, which is most often not the case. Complications and infections are frequent, driving up the costs.

Again according to Healthline, phalloplasty (a surgery to construct a functional penis in transgender men) costs "$20,000–$50,000, or even as high as $150,000." This comes after the removal of healthy breasts ($40,000). Again, complications and infections are frequent and subsequent reparative surgeries costly. It's not unusual for patients to require several reconstructions, as a functional penis is not easily obtained.[127]

I realize that the following information is very graphic and may turn your stomach, but remember, many of our young teens are accessing puberty blockers, cross-sex hormones, and other big pharma products prior to continuing on to the surgery stage. I'm keeping this as simple as possible.

During "gender affirmation surgery" [vaginoplasty], "the male external genitalia are partially removed and reconfigured. The skin of the penis and scrotum are used to create a vaginal canal and labia." This can only be accomplished if the genitalia are developed sufficiently. When children begin puberty blockers before their teen years, genital development is reduced. This creates a need for further surgery.[128]

According to the Cleveland Clinic, phalloplasty is "a complex surgery that typically requires multiple procedures...Surgeons take a large section of skin and tissue (flap) from another area of your body. After rolling it to form a shaft, they attach it to the groin." The site specifies that "tissue flaps may come from the forearm, thigh, or back."[129]

Treatment may include additional procedures to:

- Remove female genitals for patients undergoing FTM transgender surgery
- Extend the urethra (a tube through which urine leaves the body), so you can urinate while standing
- Construct a scrotum or head of the penis (glans)
- Implant a device to enable erections
- Insert artificial testicles into the scrotum[130]

"The surgery usually requires several phases to allow the constructed 'penis' to perform basic functions, such as urination." The procedure is known to have "an extremely high complication rate" (Woulahan, 2022).[131]

According to Terhune, Respaut, and Conlin, one California study found that "a quarter of 869 vaginoplasty patients" had at least one "surgical complication so severe that they had to be hospitalized.... Among those patients, 44% needed [subsequent surgeries]" to address complications such as bleeding and bowel injuries.[132]

Clinics can earn even more when you consider "hospital stays, follow-up appointments, and medications" (Woulahan, 2022).[133] Opening a gender clinic is a profitable endeavour. Across America, "thousands of [young people] are lining up for gender-affirming care" (Terhune, Respaut, and Conlin, 2022).[134]

Such surgeries have been described as butchery, even by some transgender individuals now "advocating against the procedure" (Woulahan, 2022). It is child abuse when one considers how young and vulnerable the children are when they are administered life-altering drugs that lead to surgeries. Perhaps *barbaric* is even a better word than *butchery*. Only a barbaric culture would allow such torture and abuse of its children.

It's very difficult to get good Canadian data on the number of children and young people medically transitioned because our healthcare system is managed provincially.[135] Based on data from several major gender clinics, Canada seems to be experiencing a ten-times increase in children and young people being referred for medical transition in the past ten years.[136] The BC Children's Hospital, SickKids Hospital, and CHEO (Children's Hospital of Eastern Ontario) are all reporting such increases in referrals over the past ten years.

At most clinics, the numbers of referrals are doubling every few years, if not faster than that. Further, new clinics have been created in this period. The exponential growth is unprecedented.[137] How long are we going to allow this to continue?

9

Child Sexual Abuse

9
Child Sexual Abuse

I know a thing or two about child abuse. I've experienced it personally. Then I, in my own vulnerable state, unwittingly married a pedophile.

After I remarried, I started university, studying theology and psychology jointly. I eventually earned a Ph.D. in Philosophy of Professional Counselling. For over twenty-five years I sat with sexual abuse survivors in my office. Most were systematically and chronically sexually abused throughout their childhood. You can read my story in *Damaged by the Predators Among Us*.[138]

I am an expert on child abuse. What I now see happening through and in our government-sponsored education system is systematic and chronic child abuse, applied through cunning and opportunistic governmental legislation and a corrupted educational curriculum.

Governments around the world are being forced by the United Nations Educational, Scientific, and Cultural Organization (UNESCO) to surrender to a sex education program that is sexually explicit as well as emotionally and mentally abusive. The curriculum is nothing short of pornographic.

Here is a summary of some of the World Health Organization's (WHO) International Guidelines for Sex Education[139] according to age groups:

0-4 YEARS OF AGE

- Basics of human reproduction
- Enjoyment and pleasure in touching one's body: masturbation
- Gaining awareness of gender identity: express needs, wishes, and boundaries
- Affirming that their own experience and expression of emotion is right
- Different kinds of relationships
- Talking about own relationships and family
- A positive attitude toward different lifestyles [!]
- What feels good—listen to your body
- Trust their instincts [a four-year-old's instincts?]

The WHO guidelines are all about pleasure and, in the early years, about self-stimulation and pleasuring oneself. Observing a child attempting to masturbate used to indicate that the child had early life exposure to sexual activities—for example, had been sexually assaulted or abused. These new guidelines lead to a blurring of the ability to assess child abuse.

I remind you that the guidelines above are for children four and under. What four-year-old child needs to understand human sexual reproduction? They might ask where babies come from, but a simple explanation is more than adequate. They do not need a detailed explanation of the act of intercourse at this age.

It is confusing to a normal four-year-old to discuss medical diagnoses such as gender dysphoria or identity. I remind you that the word *gender* has replaced the word *sex*. Explaining to a little boy that he has a penis and is a boy is all that is appropriate and necessary. The same goes for girls. Opposite-sex siblings in a tub together readily accept their biological differences.

I believe it is invasive of a child's privacy and basic decency to expect them to discuss their family members' sexuality and intimate relationships in class. It all sounds voyeuristic to me.

5-8-YEAR-OLDS

- Understanding, recognizing, and reducing risk of STIs, including HIV
- Choices about parenthood, pregnancy, infertility
- Adoption
- The basic idea of contraception (it is possible to plan and decide about your family)
- Enjoyment and pleasure when touching one's own body [just in case they didn't learn it in kindergarten]
- Use of sexual language in a non-offensive way

- Teaching of sexual intercourse[140]

Talk about age inappropriate. These children need to be allowed to be children without the pressures of having to learn adolescent and adult information. What eight-year-old needs to recognize STIs or HIV? By the way, here's another example of minimizing diagnostic language: STIs used to be called sexually transmitted diseases; now they're reduced to "infections," even though many are incurable.

Use of sexual language is not necessary, and neither do eight-year-olds need to understand sexual intercourse in the detail that WHO advises. In some schools, progressive teachers will use props, including plastic penises and condoms, to display how they are used. Again, what eight-year-old needs to be concerned with parenthood or pregnancy, sexual diseases, or contraception? Let our kids be kids.

9–12-YEAR-OLDS

- Both men and women can give and receive sexual pleasure
- Definition and function of orgasm
- Legal abortion performed under sterile conditions by medically trained personnel is safe [141]

I ask again, are these issues something a pre-pubescent child needs to be aware of? Explaining orgasm is totally unnecessary in any classroom, no matter the age. It leads to intrusive thoughts in the mind of the child. They already have active imaginations.

I want to give a word here about abortion. We have no abortion laws in Canada. This means that a mother can kill her baby even when it's in the birth canal. A fully developed and viable infant can be "aborted" at any stage of pregnancy or birthing. Most people are unaware of such things, but a fetus has a heartbeat by week six of gestation.[142] By weeks four to five, cells in embryo start to arrange themselves into the baby's face, brain, nose, ears, and eyes. At nine weeks, indentations appear where the baby's ears will grow, and the baby starts to hear sound around sixteen weeks. At twenty-four weeks the baby becomes more sensitive to sound, and by week twenty-five the baby responds to noise/voices in the womb.[143]

Babies in the womb are tiny humans in the process of development. Abortion stops their heartbeat, and some procedures cut them apart in the womb. I realize this is very unpleasant information, but it is truth—and a truth no child need hear or understand. Of course, teachers wouldn't discuss the actual truth about abortion, but rather the mother's right to choose (as opposed to the baby's right to live). It's all under the guise of "reproductive health," another misleading term. Many mothers have lost their lives to "legal" abortions.

One needs to think about the outcome of age-inappropriate sex education. What happens to the minds of our children? We are hypersexualizing children, opening their minds and hearts to things that they should never experience prior to adulthood—and even then it's doubtful that some of this highly sexualized curriculum is helpful.

What we are seeing in children are new levels of mental illness.

There can be several different ideas about why this is happening, but let me suggest the most obvious. Subjecting children to daily doses of sexual and pornographic materials, sex toys, and the indoctrination of a "love is love" ideology is messing with their developing brains. How on all earth can a six-year-old get their mind around the idea (and the obvious lie) that boys can be girls and girls can be boys?

No one can *ever* change their God-given biology. They can mess with it to the point of not only passing as the opposite sex, but also being medically and surgically altered to a very close representation of the opposite sex. But they can never change their bone structure and basic anatomy. They cannot change their chromosomes. In the case of a serious car accident or disease, doctors will need to know the sex of the individual in order to treat them appropriately.

Back to our children...and the outcomes we are witnessing.

- Children are being traumatized by the assertion of teachers that they can be born in the wrong body.
- Children instinctively know from the earliest ages that they are either male or female. For millenniums, our biological sex has been affirmed through cycles of reproduction, with delight and joy in the prospect of parenthood.
- Confusion reigns! The minds of our children are being tampered with. Developing brains are striving to cultivate new neuropathways to accommodate the nefarious information being fed to them. Having to focus on learning a whole new language and a new religion, while attempting

to learn the fundamentals of English, math, and history, is overwhelming and confusing.

- The education system is pitting children against their parents. While most parents have attempted to accommodate the normal development of their children, the education system is attempting to destroy all levels of biological and sexual normalcy.

- Fear and anxiety reign in the hearts and minds of our children. They are terrified of saying or doing the "wrong" thing in school or socially. What if they "misgender" someone? What if they offend someone? Children are virtually walking a tightrope every moment of every day. Young minds are not equipped to live like this.

- New levels of aggression are witnessed. Children and adolescents are lashing out at each other and their parents. They are desperate for truth—but how do they find it? This is the question that we've been trying to answer for decades, since we threw out ancient wisdom. In our attempt to become "enlightened and progressive," we have methodically lost our minds!

So where does the existing craziness take us?
Let me show you.

Up until October of 2022, in the United States alone there had been close to 270 teachers arrested on child sex-related crimes—approximately one arrest per day. Those arrested included "4 principals, 2 assistant principals, 226 teachers, 20 teacher's aides, and 17 substitute teachers," with "74% of the arrests [involving] alleged crimes against students" (Chasmar, 2022). [144]

> [A fifty-six-year-old man] who taught self-defence classes to Baltimore City Public School students was arrested...after being accused of impregnating a fourteen-year-old former student and having sexual relationships with multiple minors back to 2009, including an eight-year-old student. He [was] charged with perverted practices, second-degree rape, numerous counts of second-degree assault, and various sex offenses. (Chasmar, 2022, citing CBS News). [145]

Bear in mind that "arrests that weren't publicized were not counted in the analysis, meaning the true number may well be higher" (Chasmar, 2022).

> The number of [public education] teachers arrested for child sex abuse is just the tip of the iceberg—much as it was for the Catholic Church prior to widespread exposure and investigation in the early 2000s....The best available academic research [is] published by the Department of Education....According to that research,

the scale of sexual abuse in the public schools is **_nearly 100 times greater than that of the Catholic Church_** [emphasis mine]. (Chasmar, citing Christopher Rufo of the Manhattan Institute) [146]

According to Chasmar, Rufo had questions for "critics who seek to downplay the extent of public-school sexual abuse."

1. How many arrests need to happen before you consider it a problem?
2. How many children need to be sexually abused by teachers before you consider it a crisis?(Chasmar, 2022, citing Christopher Rufo)[147]

It is important to keep in mind that one arrest doesn't necessarily mean one offence. In fact, we know from previous research that most sex offenders, by the time they are caught, have abused dozens of children and adolescents.

For example, Chasmar reports that "a former principal, elementary school teacher, and coach who taught at-risk youth in multiple Michigan public schools…[was] accused of sexually assaulting at least fifteen boys and young adult men" over the course of several decades.[148]

In Canada our **_safe_** zones, **_safe_** spaces, **_safe_** sex, **_safe_** puberty blockers, **_safe_** cross-sex hormones, **_safe_** gender clinics, and now **_safe_** sexually explicit material in the school library have created **_confused and unsafe children_**! They are in danger.

In June of 2018, the Canadian Centre for Child Protection (C3P) released results from a study, "along with recommendations for school policies and practices to protect children." Some of the results follow; all statistics are from the 2018 *Child Sexual Abuse by K-12 School Personnel in Canada* study released by C3P. All added emphasis is mine.[149]

- 750 cases of sexual offences against a minimum of 1,272 children, carried out (or allegedly carried out) by 714 employees or former employees.
- 86% of offenders were certified teachers, but other school personnel were also charged, including educational assistants, student teachers, special needs assistants, lunch monitors, volunteers, secretaries, custodians, and school bus drivers.
- 138 offenders had another position that provided further access to children, most notably sports coaches (50%, at schools and/or in the community).
- Victims were 75% female (69% high school, 17% middle school, and 14% elementary school), and 25% male (69% high school, 20% middle school, and 11% elementary school).

According to the Canadian Center for Child Protection, "non-contact sexual abuse" is as follows:

- Encouraging a child to masturbate or watch others masturbate [being taught in our schools]

- Secretly recording or observing a child in a private situation for a sexual purpose (voyeurism)
- Exposing a child to individuals engaging in sexually explicit acts [in library and in class, sexually explicit books are readily available to our youngest children]
- Exposing a child to child-sexual abuse material [ditto]
- Flashing" or exposing genitals to a child
- Communicating over technology to make it easier to commit a specific sexual offence against a child [luring a child]
- Taking a picture or recording a video of a child's sexual organs for a sexual purpose[150]

Here's a short list of questionable books being offered to your children through their schools:

- *Crank* – Ellen Hopkins
- *The Bluest Eye* – Toni Morrison
- *The Hate U Give* – Angie Thomas
- *All Boys Aren't Blue* – George M. Johnson
- *It's Perfectly Normal* – Robie H. Harris
- *Looking for Alaska* – John Green
- *Monday's Not Coming* – Tiffany D. Jackson

PATTERNS OF SEXUAL OFFENCES

I quote from *The Prevalence of Sexual Abuse by K-12 School Personnel in Canada, 1997–2017*.[151]

Broadly defined, [a Canadian] study identified two main types of tactics employed (alone or in combination) by offenders to gain sexual access to students/children: grooming and opportunism.

[The study cites Knoll, 2010:] Grooming is "*a conscious, deliberate, and carefully orchestrated approach used by the offender*,"[152] which involves *manipulating the perceptions* of children...to gain their trust and cooperation. It is also used to *normalize inappropriate behavior through desensitization*, to reduce the likelihood that a child will disclose, and to reduce the likelihood that a child will be believed if they do tell. [Emphasis mine]

An opportunistic offender, on the other hand, is more likely to take advantage of a given situation to sexually abuse children. These offenders can take less time and have less of an emotional investment than those who groom victims and are likely to have been convicted or accused of committing one-time sexual assaults against their victim(s) (e.g., inappropriate touching).[153]

Where known...grooming behavior was identified in 70% of the cases, opportunism in 24% of the cases, luring in 4%, and the remaining 2% of cases involved some combination of these tactics.[154]

According to the report, social media and/or "technology was used in 71% of cases where grooming was the primary tactic employed....It is clear that as technology improves and becomes more readily available," it becomes more dangerous to children. Social media is being "used more often by school personnel as they seek access to students. For example, whereas technology was used by offenders only in 42% of all cases before 2010, this number rose to 60% of all cases in 2010 and after, and to 83% of all cases in 2016 and after."[155]

Parents, do you know who your child is communicating with? If you are assuming you can protect them by using a blocking device for porn sites, think again. You need to know who their teachers are and screen all messages. This, of course, will bring on the ire of your children—but better that than having them abused.

Under law, no child under twelve can consent to sexual activity, and children under sixteen can only consent to sexual activity within certain age limitations and provided there is no relationship of trust, authority, dependency, or exploitation. I don't believe that any twelve-year-old child can consent to sexual activity. Our laws need to be changed. They've left the door wide open to predators.

The "close-in-age" exceptions in section 150.1 of the *Criminal Code* supposedly seeks to permit sexual activity within sensible bounds.[156]

To return to the report, "when the ages of female victims are considered by type of school, 14% were elementary-school-aged, 17% were middle-school-aged, and 69% were high-school-aged at the time their abuse commenced."[157]

Fifty-five percent of incidents occurred on school property (including on the school bus or school trips), 29% occurred in the offender's residence and/or car, 7% occurred in the victim's residence and/or car, 3% in hotels/motels [luring], and 3% in various other public areas (most often parks).[158] (Emphasis mine.)

The vulnerable are targeted!

Seventy-five victims (60% female and 40% male) were described as having certain vulnerabilities, the most common of which included problems at home/with family (25%), personal difficulties (e.g., anxiety, depression, self-esteem issues, suffered previous abuse) (19%), having a disability/special need (18%), and substance abuse issues (10%).[159]

There is critical need for more to be done to protect children in schools across Canada.

10

Dignity, Respect,
& Identity

10

Dignity, Respect, & Identity

The word *dignity* is derived from the Latin word *dignitas*, meaning "to be worthy." Each one of us has the right to be recognized for our inherent humanity. Human dignity is a given—it's given by our Creator.

I realize that some might believe that we are the product of pond scum, which gives us absolutely no inherent dignity, but I choose to believe that we are endowed with inherent dignity because we are created in the image of God—*imago Dei*. We are set apart from the animal kingdom. We are homo sapiens—man the wise (or in some cases not so wise). We, men and women, have a highly developed, intricate ability for reason and cognitive thought.

"The moral implications of the doctrine of *imago Dei* are [quickly] apparent....If humans are to love God, then humans must love other humans, as each is an expression of God" (What Does "Imago Dei" Mean? The Image of God in the Bible, Christianity.com). Such intrinsic worth, value, and dignity is found in no other religious endeavour.

> Humans differ from all other creatures because of their
> rational structure—their capacity for deliberation and
> free decision-making. This freedom gives the human-
> centeredness and completeness which allows the
> possibility for self-actualization and participation in a
> sacred reality....The ability and desire to love one's self
> and others, and therefore, God, can become neglected
> and even opposed. Striving to bring about the *imago*
> *Dei* in one's life can be seen as the quest for wholeness,
> or one's "essential" self, as pointed to in Christ's life
> and teachings.[160]

An honouring of human dignity is deeply rooted in the Judeo-Christian ethic that we are quickly losing sight of.

It is because of a highly developed sense of self, grounded in an understanding of the image of God in us, that we then have the ability to develop a secure identity. Many events during the course of our lifetime make the path toward secure identity precarious. Nevertheless, it is up to us to develop.

Respect, unlike human dignity, is not an instantaneous event. Respect is to be earned. The Latin word for *respect* is *respectus*, meaning "to look back at." Respect is the desire to show admiration for someone because of their abilities, qualities, or achievements.

When I ponder on the image of Kayla Lemieux, I find it difficult to garner any sense of respect for this person. While Kayla has human dignity that I believe he/she is trying to destroy, that does not mean that Kayla automatically gains my respect.

Our society, though, requires respect and dignity to be merged together to enable equal inclusion. This "word sandwich" does nothing to clarify and everything to confuse. The idea is that inclusion, particularly the inclusion of all sexual beliefs and practices, will create dignity and respect. Nothing could be further from the truth. The reality is we have a generation that is filled with self-hatred, rejection of their bodies, and deep rage as a result of being served a daily diet of deception.

Deceit and betrayal have done nothing to uphold humanity's inherent sense of worth and dignity—their *imago Dei*—but instead have created a deep void of insecurity, anxiety, depression, and self-contempt that has led us to the pinnacle of the greatest mental health crisis the world has ever known.

I see only one way to bring us back from the brink of destruction. It is to turn our hearts and minds to once again embrace our humanity with the existential reality of our creation—to embrace once again our Judeo-Christian ethic, and restore our relationship with the Creator of all.

references

Abrams, M., 2018. Top Surgery: Cost, Recovery, and Procedure Details. Healthline.com.

Alston, L., n.d. What is Lithromantic? rideable.org/what-is-lithromantic/

American Psychiatric Association, 1980. Diagnostic and Statistical Manual of Mental Disorders (3rd ed.). Washington, D.C.: Author.

American Psychiatric Association, 2013. Diagnostic and statistical manual of mental disorders (5th ed.). Washington, DC: Author.

BabyHeart Australia, n.d. Fetal Heartbeat By Week Chart.

Bakunyuu 爆乳

Bilek, J., 2022. The Pritzker Family, the Capture of Yale University and the Marketing of Synthetic Sex to Children (the11thhourblog.com)

Blom, R.M., Guglielmi, V., and Denys, D., 2016. Elective amputation of a "healthy limb." *CNS Spectrums* 21(5), 360–361. https://doi.org/10.1017/S1092852916000456

Botelho, G., 2015. Rachel Dolezal, ex-NAACP leader: "I identify as black" | CNN

Bou Khalil, R., and Richa, S., December 2012. Apotemnophilia or body integrity identity disorder: a case report review. *The International Journal of Lower Extremity Wounds* 11(4).

Brandt, J., Prescott, D.S., and Wilson, R.J., 2012. Sexual Abuse: Pornography and Contact Offending (atsa.com)

Brugger, P., and Lenggenhager, B., December 2014. The bodily self and its disorders: neurological, psychological and social aspects. *Current Opinion in Neurology* 27(6): 644–52.

Butler and Grace Ltd., 2018. LGBT+ colours and their meanings.

Camp Ernst Middle School, 2021. CEMS - #CEMSBlazers | Facebook

Canadian Centre for Child Protection Inc., 2018. The Prevalence of Sexual Abuse by K-12 School Personnel in Canada, 1997–2017. *Journal of Child Sexual Abuse* 28(1); Taylor and Francis Online (tandfonline.com)

Canadian Centre for Child Protection, n.d. Resources & Research: Child Sexual Abuse by K–12 School Personnel in Canada. protectchildren.ca.

Canadian Gender Report, 2021. 10x growth in referrals to gender clinics in Canada and our "consent" based model.

Cash, B.M., 2016. "Self-Identifications, Sexual Development, and Wellbeing in Minor-Attracted People: An Exploratory Study" (master's thesis). Cornell University, Ithaca, NY.

Centers for Disease Control and Prevention, 2010. Sexually Transmitted Disease surveillance 2009. Atlanta: U.S. Department of Health and Human Services.

Chasmar, J., 2022. At least 269 K-12 educators arrested on child sex crimes in first 9 months of this year. https://www.foxnews.com/politics/

Chelette, R., 2023. Are We Killing Our Kids? www.livehope.org/article/are-we-killing-our-kids/

Christianity.com Editorial Staff, 2022. What Does "Imago Dei" Mean in the Bible? What is the Image of God? Christianity.com

Clary, S., 2018. Bottom Surgery: Cost, Recovery, Procedure Details, and More. Healthline.com.

Clevelandclinic.org, 2021. Phalloplasty: What is it, Risks, Benefits, Recovery and Outlook.

Clevelandclinic.org, 2021. Vaginoplasty: Procedure Details, Risks, Benefits and Recovery.

Clowes, B., 2022. How many people are homosexuals? Human Life International. Homosexuality: Gay, Lesbian, and Bisexual Demographics in the US (hli. org), p. 6.

Dana-Farber Cancer Institute, 2021. Young women with breast cancer who opt for mastectomies report lower quality of life (medicalxpress.com)

Davydovskaya, Y., 2022. Lupron Depot. Medical News Today.

Definitions.net. Straight Ally.

Diamant, A.L., Wold, C., Spritzer, K., and Gelberg, L., 2000. Health behaviors, health status, and access to and use of health care: A population-based study of lesbian, bisexual, and heterosexual women. *Archives of Family Medicine* 9, 1043–1051.

Dictionary.com. Demiromantic

Dictionary.com/Gender & Sexuality Dictionary. Polysexual; Skoliosexual.

DuBay, W. H., 2001. Homosexuality: What Kinsey Really Said. http://www. queerbychoice.com/dubay_homosexuality.html

Duggan, L., 2022. Number of Pediatric "Gender Clinics" Exploding Across the Country (westernjournal.com)

First, M.B., 2005. Desire for amputation of a limb: paraphilia, psychosis, or a new type of identity disorder. *Psychol Med* 35(6):919–928.

First, M.B., and Fisher, C.E., 2012. Body integrity identity disorder: the persistent desire to acquire a physical disability. *Psychopathology* 45(1), 3–14. https:// doi.org/10.1159/000330503

Freimond, C.M. (2009). "Navigating the Stigma of Pedophilia: The Experiences of Nine Minor-Attracted Men in Canada" (master's thesis). Simon Fraser University, British Columbia, Canada.

Frisch, M., and Brønnum-Hansen, H., 2009. Mortality among men and women in same-sex marriage: A national cohort study of 8333 Danes. *American Journal of Public Health* 99(1), 133–137.

Frisch, M., Smith, E., Grulich, A., and Johansen, C., 2003. Cancer in a population-based cohort of men and women in registered homosexual partnerships. *American Journal of Epidemiology* 157, 966–972.

Gender Wiki/Fandom. Neutrois.

Gillies, A.E., 2016. An Exploration of a Sample of Christian Men Experiencing Same-Sex Attraction (researchgate.net).

Gillies, A.E., 2017. *Closing the Floodgates: Setting the Record Straight on Gender and Sexuality*. Winnipeg, Manitoba, Canada: Word Alive Publishing.

Gillies, A.E., 2022. *Damaged by the Predators Among Us*. Independently published. https://www.amazon.com/Damaged-Predators-Among-Gillies-Ph-D/

Goode, S., 2010. *Understanding and Addressing Adult Sexual Attraction to Children: A study of paedophiles in contemporary society*. Oxford, UK: Routledge.

HALT (Humanity Against Local Terrorism), 2012. Child sexual abuse statistics. http://haltnow.ca/what-is-abuse/child-sexual-abuse/child-sexual-abuse-statistics

Hodge, M., 2020. How Jeffrey Epstein learned his vile grooming techniques while working as "creepy" Math teacher before being sacked – The Sun | The Sun

Hogg, R.S., Strathdee, S.A., Craib, K.J., O'Shaughnessy, M.V., Montaner, J.S., and Schechter, M.T., 1997. Modelling the impact of HIV disease on mortality in gay and bisexual men. *International Journal of Epidemiology* 26(3), 657–661.

Holt, K., Kissinger, J., Spickler, C., and Roush, V., 2021. Pornography Use and Sexual Offending: An Examination of Perceptions of Role and Risk - PubMed (nih.gov)

ICD-11 for Mortality and Morbidity Statistics, 2023. Gender Incongruence. https://icd.who.int/browse11/l-m/en#/http://id.who.int/icd/entity/411470068

International Anthropomorphic Research Project. What are furries? Furscience.com

Justin, 2021. Akoiromantic: When You Love But Don't Want to Be Loved in Return. lbibinders.org/akoiromantic/

Kandola, A., 2021. What does nonbinary mean? www.medicalnewstoday.com/articles

Kay, J., 2022. The Canadian Gender-Rights Movement Enters Its Hentai Phase.

Kinsey, A.C., Pomeroy, W.P., and Martin, C. E. (1948). *Sexual Behavior in the Human Male*. Bloomington, IN: Indiana University Press.

Kinsey, A.C., Pomeroy, W.P., and Martin, C.E., 1948. *Sexual Behavior in the Human Male*. Bloomington, IN: Indiana University Press.

Knoll, J., 2010. "Teacher sexual misconduct: Grooming patterns and female offenders," in *Journal of Child Sexual Abuse*, 19(4), 371–386.

Leaf, C., 2015. *Switch on Your Brain*. Grand Rapids, MI: Baker Books.

leatherpup.me/2017/11/22/the-benefits-of-regular-chores-in-a-d-s/

LifeXchange, n.d. Neural Pathways: How Your Mind Stores the Info and Thoughts that Affect Your Behaviour (lifexchangesolutions.com)

Lines, C., 2021. Four in five UK 16- and 17-year-olds have seen online pornography, most commonly on the day of the survey. City, University of London website.

McIlhaney, J.S., Jr., and Bush, F.M., 2008. *Hooked: New Science on How Casual Sex Is Affecting Our Children*. Chicago: Moody.

Merriam-Webster. *Androgynous; Anime; Pansexual; Paraphilia; Transsexual.*

Metro Weekly. Puppy Love. (archive.org)

Moser, C., 2010. Blanchard's Autogynephilia Theory: a critique. *Journal of homosexuality*, 57(6), 790–809. https://doi.org/10.1080/00918369.2010. 486241

Newman, A., 2022. Brainwashed School Kids Now Identifying as Animal "Furries." The New American.

O'Keefe Osborn, C., 2018. Vaginoplasty: Gender Confirmation Surgery Risks and Recovery. Healthline.com.

Ontario College of Teachers, 2021. Hearings. professionallyspeaking.oct.ca

Parker, J., 2023. "Leave them kids alone," sang Pink Floyd in 1979. Now it's: "we'll convert your children." Sex & Society, MercatorNet. mercatornet.com/aus-worldpride-2023-convert-children/83340/

Pearson, A., November 4, 2017. What is a "Bear" in Gay Culture? (michianaglbtcenter.org). GLBT Resource of Michiana.

Pedersen, M.R., 2017. "The Politics of being a Pedophile." https://www.b4uact. org/wp-content/uploads/2014/12/The-Politics-of-being-a-Pedophile.pdf

Pereda, N., and Gallardo-Pujol, D., 2011. Neurobiological consequences of child sexual abuse: a systematic review. *Gaceta sanitaria* 25(3), 233–239. https:// doi.org/10.1016/j.gaceta.2010.12.004. PubMed (nih.gov).

Pilastro, E., 2022. "I did it for me": Meet the man with 516 body modifications | Guinness World Records

PubMed (nih.gov). Pornography Use and Sexual Offending: An Examination of Perceptions of Role and Risk.

Reisman, J., and Eichel, E.W., 1990. *Kinsey, Sex, and Fraud: The Indoctrination of a People*. Lafayette, LA: Lochinvar-Huntington House.

Reyes, R., 2022. Canadian high school...refusing to address parents' concerns. https://www.dailymail.co.uk/

Rocca, R., 2022. Oakville teacher controversy: Professional standards under review by Ontario College of Teachers | Globalnews.ca

Sara McGrath on Twitter: Four teenagers in a detransition support group asked how long it would take for their breasts to grow back. / Twitter

Sedda, A., and Bottini, G., 2014. Apotemnophilia, body integrity identity disorder or xenomelia? Psychiatric and neurologic etiologies face each other. *Neuropsychiatric disease and treatment* 10, 1255–1265. https://doi.org/10.2147/NDT.S53385

Skeid, S., 2018. WHO takes bdsm and fetishism off the sick list - Revise F65. revisef65.net.

Slatz, A., 2022. Ontario High School Teacher Seen Wearing Massive Prosthetic Bust to Class. Reduxx.

Terhune, C., Respaut, R., and Conlin, M., 2022. As more transgender children seek medical care, families confront many unknowns. https://www.reuters.com/investigates/special-report/usa-transyouth-care/

Timmons, J., 2018. When Can a Fetus Hear: Womb Development Timeline. Healthline.com.

Trans Care BC: Provincial Health Services Authority, n.d. Puberty Blockers for Youth (phsa.ca)

University and College Union (UCU), 2019. Statement reaffirming UCU's commitment trans inclusion.

University and College Union (UCU), n.d. Equality.

Urban Dictionary.com. *Apromantic; Demiromantic; Grey-romantic.*

Walsh, M., n.d. What is a Woman? | The Daily Wire

Warmington, J., 2022. Oakville trans teacher allowed to dress any way she likes | Toronto Sun

Weiss, R., n.d. Raised on Porn | Documentary Film - YouTube

Wikipedia. Jeffrey Epstein.

WLWT Digital Staff, 2021. Students barking, acting like dogs at Burlington middle school. wlwt.com

World Health Organization, 2018. International technical guidance on sexuality education. An evidence-informed approach. who.int.

Woulahan, S., 2022. "Big Money Makers": Nashville Gender Clinic Boasts of Gender Surgery Profits - Reduxx

Yanchus, K., 2022. Oakville high school parents taking legal action against Halton District School Board. The Record.com.

Zambon, V., 2021. What are puberty blockers? Medical News Today

notes

1 Botelho, G., 2015. Rachel Dolezal, ex-NAACP leader: 'I identify as black' | CNN

2 University and College Union (UCU), n.d. Statement reaffirming UCU's commitment trans inclusion.

3 University and College Union (UCU), n.d. Statement reaffirming UCU's commitment trans inclusion.

4 University and College Union, n.d. Equality.

5 Gay Definition & Meaning - Merriam-Webster

6 Gay Definition & Meaning - Merriam-Webster

7 Frisch, Smith, Grulich, and Johansen, 2003. Cancer in a population-based cohort of men and women in registered homosexual partnerships. *American Journal of Epidemiology* 157, 966–972.

8 Diamant, Wold, Spritzer, and Gelberg, 2000. Health behaviors, health status, and access to and use of health care: A population-based study of lesbian, bisexual, and heterosexual women. *Archives of Family Medicine* 9, 1043–1051.

9 Centers for Disease Control and Prevention, 2010. Sexually Transmitted Disease surveillance 2009. Atlanta: U.S. Department of Health and Human Services.

10 Hogg, R.S., Strathdee, S.A., Craib, K.J., O'Shaughnessy, M.V., Montaner, J.S., and Schechter, M.T., 1997. Modelling the impact of HIV disease on mortality in gay and bisexual men. *International Journal of Epidemiology* 26(3), 657–661.

11 Frisch and Brønnum-Hansen, 2009. Mortality among men and women in same-sex marriage: A national cohort study of 8333 Danes. *American Journal of Public Health* 99(1), 133–137.

12 Butler and Grace Ltd., 2018. LGBT+ colours and their meanings.

13 Butler and Grace Ltd., 2018. LGBT+ colours and their meanings..

14 Butler and Grace Ltd., 2018. LGBT+ colours and their meanings.

15 Chelette, R., 2023. Are We Killing Our Kids? www.livehope.org/article/are-we-killing-our-kids/

16 Androphilia Flag | Rocky Mountain Flag Company

17 https://www.merriam-webster.com/dictionary/androgynous

18 Autosexual - LGBTQIA+ Wiki

19 https://www.rd.com/list/lgbtq-flags/

20 sadism - definition and meaning (wordnik.com)

21 https://www.wordnik.com/words/masochism

22 BDSM Definition & Meaning - Merriam-Webster

23 Kink (sexuality) - Wikipedia

24 https://www.dictionary.com/browse/demiromantic

25 Kandola, A., 2021. What does nonbinary mean? www.medicalnewstoday.com/articles

26 Reisman and Eichel, 1990. *Kinsey, Sex, and Fraud: The Indoctrination of a People.* Lafayette, LA: Lochinvar-Huntington House.

27 Kinsey, 1948, cited in DuBay, 2001. Homosexuality: What Kinsey Really Said. http://www.queerbychoice.com/dubay_homosexuality.html

28 Clowes, B., 2022. How many people are homosexuals? Human Life International. Homosexuality: Gay, Lesbian, and Bisexual Demographics in the US (hli.org),p. 6

29 Gillies, A.E., 2017. *Closing the Floodgates: Setting the Record Straight on Gender and Sexuality.* Winnipeg, Manitoba: Word Alive Press.

30 Grey-romantic - LGBTQIA+ Wiki

31 lipstick lesbian - Wiktionary

32   Neutrois | Gender Wiki | Fandom

33   https://www.merriam-webster.com/dictionary/pansexual

34   polysexual Meaning | Gender & Sexuality | Dictionary.com

35   The Polyamorous Flag Meaning and Reasons It Was Created (flagwix.com)

36   https://www.dictionary.com/e/gender-sexuality/skoliosexual/

37   https://www.definitions.net/definition/straight+ally

38   https://www.definitions.net/definition/straight+ally

39   Transsexual Definition & Meaning - Merriam-Webster

40   Sexuality Flags & LGBT+ Symbols: The Ultimate Pride Guide (vispronet.com)

41   Twink (gay slang) - Wikipedia

42   American Psychiatric Association, 2013. Diagnostic and Statistical Manual of Mental Disorders (5th ed.).

43   American Psychiatric Association, 2013. Diagnostic and Statistical Manual of Mental Disorders (5th ed.).

44   American Psychiatric Association, 1980. Diagnostic and Statistical Manual of Mental Disorders (3rd ed.).

45   Skeid, S., 2018. "WHO takes bdsm and fetishism off the sick list - Revise F65". revisef65.net.

46   ICD-11 for Mortality and Morbidity Statistics, 2023. Gender Incongruence. https://icd.who.int/browse11/l-m/en#/http://id.who.int/icd/entity/411470068

47   ICD-11 for Mortality and Morbidity Statistics, 2023. Gender Incongruence. https://icd.who.int/browse11/l-m/en#/http://id.who.int/icd/entity/411470068

48   ICD-11 for Mortality and Morbidity Statistics, 2023. Gender Incongruence. https://icd.who.int/browse11/l-m/en#/http://id.who.int/icd/entity/411470068

49   American Psychiatric Association, 2013. Diagnostic and Statistical Manual of Mental Disorders (5th ed.).

50   American Psychiatric Association, 2013. Diagnostic and Statistical Manual of Mental Disorders (5th ed.).

51   Moser, C., 2010. Blanchard's Autogynephilia Theory: a critique - PubMed (nih.gov)

52   Ray Blanchard - Wikipedia

53   Ray Blanchard - Wikipedia

54   American Psychiatric Association, 2013. Diagnostic and Statistical Manual of Mental Disorders (5th ed.).

55   American Psychiatric Association, 2013. Diagnostic and Statistical Manual of Mental Disorders (5th ed.).

56   American Psychiatric Association, 2013. Diagnostic and Statistical Manual of Mental Disorders (5th ed.).

57   American Psychiatric Association, 2013. Diagnostic and Statistical Manual of Mental Disorders (5th ed.)..

58   Parker, J., 2023. "Leave them kids alone," sang Pink Floyd in 1979. Now it's: "we'll convert your children." Sex & Society, MercatorNet. mercatornet.com/aus-worldpride-2023-convert-children/83340/

59   Warmington, J., 2022. Oakville trans teacher allowed to dress any way she likes | Toronto Sun; Slatz, A., 2022. Ontario High School Teacher Seen Wearing Massive Prosthetic Bust to Class. Reduxx.

60   Reyes, R., 2022. Canadian high school...refusing to address parents' concerns. DailyMail.com; Yanchus, K., 2022. Oakville High school parents...against Halton District School Board. The Record.com/.

61   Kay, J., 2022. The Canadian Gender-Rights Movement Enters Its Hentai Phase; Bakunyuu 爆乳

62   Kay, J., 2022. The Canadian Gender-Rights Movement Enters Its Hentai Phase

63   Merriam-Webster. Paraphilia Definition & Meaning.

64   Rocca, R., 2022. Oakville teacher controversy: Professional standards under review by Ontario College of Teachers | Globalnews.ca

65   HALT (Humanity Against Local Terrorism), 2012. Child sexual abuse statistics. http://haltnow.ca/what-is-abuse/child-sexual-abuse/child-sexual-abuse-statistics

66   Ontario College of Teachers, 2021. Hearings. professionallyspeaking.oct.ca

67   Ontario College of Teachers, 2021.

68   Lines, C., 2021. "Four in five UK 16- and 17-year-olds have seen online pornography, most commonly on the day of the survey." City, University of London website.

69   Lines, C., 2021. "Four in five UK 16- and 17-year-olds have seen online pornography, most commonly on the day of the survey." City, University of London website.

70   Weiss, R., n.d. Raised on Porn | Documentary Film - YouTube

71   McIlhaney and Bush, 2008. *Hooked: New Science on How Casual Sex Is Affecting Our Children*. Chicago: Moody.

72   Pereda, N., and Gallardo-Pujol, D., 2011. Neurobiological consequences of child sexual abuse: a systematic review. PubMed (nih.gov)

73   Leaf, C., 2015. *Switch on Your Brain*. Grand Rapids, MI: Baker Books.

74   LifeXchange, n.d. Neural Pathways: How Your Mind Stores the Info and Thoughts that Affect Your Behaviour (lifexchangesolutions.com)

75   Gillies, A.E., 2022. *Damaged by the Predators Among Us*.

76   Holt, K., Kissinger, J., Spickler, C., and Roush, V., 2021. Pornography Use and Sexual Offending: An Examination of Perceptions of Role and Risk - PubMed (nih.gov)

77   Brandt, J., Prescott, D.S., and Wilson, R.J., 2012. Sexual Abuse: Pornography and Contact Offending (atsa.com)

78   Brandt, J., Prescott, D.S., and Wilson, R.J., 2012. Sexual Abuse: Pornography and Contact Offending (atsa.com).

79   Newman, A., 2022. Brainwashed School Kids Now Identifying as Animal "Furries." The New American.

80   Private communicate from a former teacher.

81   WLWT, 2021. Students barking, acting like dogs at Burlington middle school (wlwt.com)

82   International Anthropomorphic Research Project.

83   Merriam-Webster. Anime Definition and Meaning.

84   International Anthropomorphic Research Project.

85   International Anthropomorphic Research Project.

86   Camp Ernst Middle School - CEMS - #CEMSBlazers | Facebook.

87   Camp Ernst Middle School - CEMS - #CEMSBlazers | Facebook

88   Metro Weekly, n.d. Puppy Love.

89   Metro Weekly, n.d. Puppy Love.

90   leatherpup.me/2017/11/22/the-benefits-of-regular-chores-in-a-d-s/

91   leatherpup.me/2017/11/22/the-benefits-of-regular-chores-in-a-d-s/

92   leatherpup.me/2017/11/22/the-benefits-of-regular-chores-in-a-d-s/

93   leatherpup.me/2017/11/22/the-benefits-of-regular-chores-in-a-d-s/

94   Hodge, M., 2020. How Jeffrey Epstein learned his vile grooming techniques while working as 'creepy' Math teacher before being sacked – The Sun | The Sun

95   Wikipedia. Jeffrey Epstein.

96   Wikipedia. Jeffrey Epstein.

97   Wikipedia. Jeffrey Epstein.

98   Pedersen, 2017. The Politics of being a Pedophile. b4uact.org.

99   Freimond, 2009. Navigating the Stigma of Pedophilia (master's thesis); Goode, 2010. *Understanding and Addressing Adult Sexual Attraction to Children.* Oxford, UK: Routledge.

100   Goode, 2010; Freimond, 2009; Cash, 2016. Self-Identifications, Sexual Development, and Wellbeing in Minor-Attracted People (master's thesis); Pedersen, 2017.

101   Reisman, J., and Eichel, E.W., 1990.

102   Pilastro, E., 2022. "I did it for me": Meet the man with 516 body modifications | Guinness World Records

103   Dana-Farber Cancer Institute, 2021. Young women with breast cancer who opt for mastectomies report lower quality of life (medicalxpress.com)

104   Sara McGrath on Twitter: "Four teenagers in a detransition support group asked how long it would take for their breasts to grow back." / Twitter

105   Sedda and Botini, 2014. Apotemnophilia, body integrity identity disorder or xenomelia? Psychiatric and neurologic etiologies face each other - PubMed (nih.gov)

106 First, M.B., and Fisher, C.E., 2012. Body integrity identity disorder: the persistent desire to acquire a physical disability. *Psychopathology* 45(1): 3–14.

107 Sedda and Botini, 2014. Apotemnophilia, body integrity identity disorder or xenomelia? Psychiatric and neurologic etiologies face each other - PubMed (nih.gov)

108 Brugger, P., and Lenggenhager, B., December 2014. The bodily self and its disorders: neurological, psychological and social aspects. Current Opinion in Neurology 27 (6): 644–52.

109 Blom, R.M., Guglielmi, V., and Denys, D., 2016. Elective amputation of a "healthy limb" - PubMed (nih.gov)

110 Bou Khalil, R., and Richa, S., December 2012. Apotemnophilia or body integrity identity disorder: a case report review. *The International Journal of Lower Extremity Wounds* 11 (4).

111 Bou Khalil, R., and Richa, S., December 2012. Apotemnophilia or body integrity identity disorder: a case report review. *The International Journal of Lower Extremity Wounds* 11 (4).

112 First, M.B., 2005. Desire for amputation of a limb: paraphilia, psychosis, or a new type of identity disorder. *Psychol Med* 35(6):919–928.

113 First, M.B., 2005. Desire for amputation of a limb: paraphilia, psychosis, or a new type of identity disorder. *Psychol Med* 35(6):919–928.

114 Bilek, J., 2022. The Pritzker Family, the Capture of Yale University and the Marketing of Synthetic Sex to Children (the11thhourblog.com)

115 Bilek, J., 2022. The Pritzker Family, the Capture of Yale University and the Marketing of Synthetic Sex to Children (the11thhourblog.com).

116 Woulahan, S., 2022. "Big Money Makers": Nashville Gender Clinic Boasts of Gender Surgery Profits - Reduxx

117 Walsh, M., n.d. What is a Woman? | The Daily Wire

118 Woulahan, S., 2022. "Big Money Makers": Nashville Gender Clinic Boasts of Gender Surgery Profits - Reduxx

119 Woulahan, S., 2022. "Big Money Makers": Nashville Gender Clinic Boasts of Gender Surgery Profits - Reduxx

120   Zambon, V., 2021. What are puberty blockers? Medical News Today. https://www.medicalnewstoday.com/articles/puberty-blockers#what-are-they

121   Trans Care BC, n.d. Puberty Blockers for Youth (phsa.ca) Provincial Health Services Authority.

122   Davydovskaya, Y., 2022. Lupron Depot. Medical News Today.

123   Duggan, L., 2022. Number of Pediatric 'Gender Clinics' Exploding Across the Country (westernjournal.com)

124   Terhune, Respaut, and Conlin, 2022. As more transgender children seek medical care, families confront many unknowns. www.reuters.com/investigates/special-report/usa-transyouth-care/

125   Abrams, M., 2018. Top Surgery: Cost, Recovery, and Procedure Details (healthline.com)

126   O'Keefe Osborn, 2018. Vaginoplasty: Gender Confirmation Surgery Risks and Recovery (healthline.com)

127   Clary, S., 2018. Bottom Surgery: Cost, Recovery, Procedure Details, and More (healthline.com); Cleveland Clinic, 2021. Phalloplasty. my.clevelandclinic.org/health/treatments/phalloplasty

128   Cleveland Clinic, 2021. Vaginoplasty: Procedure Details, Risks, Benefits & Recovery (clevelandclinic.org)

129   Cleveland Clinic, 2021. Phalloplasty: What is it, Risks, Benefits, Recovery & Outlook (clevelandclinic.org)

130   Cleveland Clinic, 2021. Phalloplasty: What is it, Risks, Benefits, Recovery & Outlook (clevelandclinic.org)

131   Woulahan, S., 2022. "Big Money Makers": Nashville Gender Clinic Boasts of Gender Surgery Profits - Reduxx

132   Terhune, Respaut, and Conlin, 2022. As more transgender children seek medical care, families confront many unknowns. www.reuters.com/investigates/special-report/usa-transyouth-care/.

133   Woulahan, S., 2022. "Big Money Makers": Nashville Gender Clinic Boasts of Gender Surgery Profits - Reduxx

134 Terhune, Respaut, and Conlin, 2022. As more transgender children seek medical care, families confront many unknowns. www.reuters.com/ investigates/special-report/usa-transyouth-care/

135 Canadian Gender Report, 2021. 10x growth in referrals to gender clinics in Canada and our "consent" based model.

136 Canadian Gender Report, 2021. 10x growth in referrals to gender clinics in Canada and our "consent" based model..

137 Canadian Gender Report, 2021. 10x growth in referrals to gender clinics in Canada and our "consent" based model.

138 https://www.amazon.ca/Damaged-Predators-Among-Gillies-Ph-D/dp/ B0BP495VHF/

139 Adapted from International technical guidance on sexuality education. An evidence-informed approach (who.int)

140 International technical guidance on sexuality education. An evidence-informed approach (who.int)

141 International technical guidance on sexuality education. An evidence-informed approach (who.int)

142 BabyHeart, Australia, n.d. Fetal Heartbeat By Week Chart | BabyHeart

143 Timmons, J., 2018. When Can a Fetus Hear: Womb Development Timeline (healthline.com)

144 Chasmar, J., 2022. https://www.foxnews.com/politics/at-least-269-k-12-educators-arrested-child-sex-crimes-first-9-months-year

145 Chasmar, J., 2022. https://www.foxnews.com/politics/at-least-269-k-12-educators-arrested-child-sex-crimes-first-9-months-year

146 Chasmar, J., 2022. https://www.foxnews.com/politics/at-least-269-k-12-educators-arrested-child-sex-crimes-first-9-months-year

147 Chasmar, J., 2022. https://www.foxnews.com/politics/at-least-269-k-12-educators-arrested-child-sex-crimes-first-9-months-year

148 Chasmar, J., 2022. https://www.foxnews.com/politics/at-least-269-k-12-educators-arrested-child-sex-crimes-first-9-months-year

149   Canadian Centre for Child Protection, n.d. Resources & Research: Child Sexual Abuse by K–12 School Personnel in Canada.

150   Canadian Centre for Child Protection, n.d. Home – protectchildren.ca

151   Canadian Centre for Child Protection, Inc., 2018. The Prevalence of Sexual Abuse by K-12 School Personnel in Canada, 1997–2017 (tandfonline.com), citing Shakeshaft, C., 2013.Know the warning signs of educator sexual misconduct. *Phi Delta Kappan*, 94(5), 8–13.

152   Canadian Centre for Child Protection, Inc., 2018. The Prevalence of Sexual Abuse by K-12 School Personnel in Canada, 1997–2017 (tandfonline.com), citing Knoll, 2010 (p. 374). "Teacher sexual misconduct: Grooming patterns and female offenders," in *Journal of Child Sexual Abuse*, 19(4), 371–386.

153   Canadian Centre for Child Protection, Inc., 2018. The Prevalence of Sexual Abuse by K-12 School Personnel in Canada, 1997–2017 (tandfonline.com).

154   Canadian Centre for Child Protection, Inc., 2018. The Prevalence of Sexual Abuse by K-12 School Personnel in Canada, 1997–2017 (tandfonline.com).

155   Canadian Centre for Child Protection, Inc., 2018. The Prevalence of Sexual Abuse by K-12 School Personnel in Canada, 1997–2017 (tandfonline.com)

156   Canadian Centre for Child Protection, Inc., 2018. The Prevalence of Sexual Abuse by K-12 School Personnel in Canada, 1997–2017 (tandfonline.com)

157   Canadian Centre for Child Protection, Inc., 2018. The Prevalence of Sexual Abuse by K-12 School Personnel in Canada, 1997–2017 (tandfonline.com)

158   Canadian Centre for Child Protection, Inc., 2018. The Prevalence of Sexual Abuse by K-12 School Personnel in Canada, 1997–2017 (tandfonline.com)

159   Canadian Centre for Child Protection, Inc., 2018. The Prevalence of Sexual Abuse by K-12 School Personnel in Canada, 1997–2017 (tandfonline.com).

160   Christianity.com. What Does "Imago Dei" Mean in the Bible? What is the Image of God?

Manufactured by Amazon.ca
Bolton, ON